RICK GEKOSKI is an Americ. post-graduate work at Oxford. After finishing his PhD in English, he taught at the University of Warwick until 1984. In 1982, he started his rare-books business, dealing in important twentieth-century first editions and manuscripts. Rick has worked as a publisher, critic, bibliographer and broadcaster (his BBC Radio series *Rare Books, Rare People* was acclaimed by the *Telegraph* as 'one of the gems of Radio 4'). He is also the author of *Joseph Conrad: The Moral World of the Novelist*, *William Golding: A Bibliography* (with P.A. Grogan) and *Staying Up: A Fan Behind the Scenes in the Premiership*. Rick was one of the 2005 Booker Prize judges.

'A fascinating backstage look at his own rare-book trade, with some memorably bizarre encounters with literary giants.'
Selina Hastings, *Sunday Telegraph* Books of the Year 2004

'Page after page of delight.' *Sunday Times*

'Book aficionados will be titillated by Gekoski's wealth of inside knowledge and tasty gossip morsels.' *Financial Times*

'Gekoski's judgments are always interesting . . . his reminiscences of authors and collectors priceless.' *Rare Book Review*

'Rick Gekoski [is] a modern-first dealer who has dragged many a huge beast of a book back from the jungle and brought it blinking in the spotlight like a 40ft ape.' *Guardian*

'No lover of fiction will want to miss out on the skeletons in these closets.' *Big Issue*

'A veritable feast of the tales behind some of the most iconic titles to have graced British publishing, and fascinating anecdotes about the authors who wrote them . . . Tolkien, Potter, Orwell,

Larkin, Hemingway and more, representing a treasure trove of trivia for book fans. Really, every library should have one!'

'An irresistible collection of stories and anecdotes.'

'A pure pleasure.'

'Rick Gekoski's love of books is infectious. He makes you want to revisit the books worth reading, or at least, appreciate the dusty tomes on your bookshelf you had forgotten about.' *Seattle Times*

'Wildly readable . . . irresistible.'

'There is something about Rick Gekoski that is larger than life. It may not be strictly English trade practice but certainly adds to the gaiety of the nation.' *Book Collector*

'Riveting and entertaining. I couldn't put it down.' *Australian*

'A treasure trove . . . A bibliophile's delight.' *New Zealand Herald*

'Beautifully produced, entertaining, thought-provoking.'

'You couldn't ask for a more entertaining guide than Gekoski, who sparkles with laughter and sheer relish.'

'I would nominate Rick for Best Memoir, by a long shot. His chapters . . . breathe fresh air into what have been very stagnant waters for way too long.'

for Graham Greene
November 1959
from Vladimir Nabokov

LOLITA

"green swallowtail dancing waisthigh"

For Virginia Woolf.
from the author.
T.S. Eliot

Tolkien's
Gown & Other
Stories of Great
Authors and Rare Books

For Harold —
remembering his kindness
in enabling me to have
net practice
with Trinidad reg
+
Philip

For Rick Gekoski
with best wishes
from William Golding

Rick Gekoski

To Rick, this copy no. II
from the owner of no. I —
Best wishes,

SALMAN RUSHDIE

THE
SATANIC
VERSES

For Nick Gekoski;
A book which won't like!
from Graham Greene.
Nov. 18 '88

CONSTABLE · LONDON

For Graham Greene
this antiquated work
from Evelyn Waugh

THIS BOOK
IS FOR HADLEY
and this one is for
Edward J. O'Brien
from Ernest Hemingway

For Belinda

Constable & Robinson Ltd
3 The Lanchesters
162 Fulham Palace Road
London W6 9ER
www.constablerobinson.com

Published in the UK by Constable
an imprint of Constable & Robinson Ltd 2004

This paperback edition published by Constable,
an imprint of Constable & Robinson Ltd 2005

By arrangement with the BBC

B B C © BBC 1996

A copy of the British Library Cataloguing in
Publication Data is available from the British Library

ISBN 1-84529-239-1 (pbk)
ISBN 1-84119-929-X (hbk)

Printed and bound in the EU

3 5 7 9 10 8 6 4 2

Acknowledgements

This book derives from a BBC Radio 4 series entitled *Rare Books, Rare People*, and I am grateful to my producers Lisa Osbourne and Ivan Howlett for their patience and instruction, and to Peter Hoare of Pier Productions for his encouragement.

In rewriting the material, and in adding to it, I have been lovingly edited by Carol O'Brien, at Constable & Robinson, and had hugely helpful research assistance from Elinor Hodgson. Peter Grogan, Peter Straus and Paul Rassam have generously helped me to avoid errors of fact and judgement, and infelicities of expression. I would like to thank Clive Hirschhorn, Natalie Galustian, Pom Harrington and Geordie Williamson, who helped assemble the photographs of the books.

I am grateful to Faber and Faber for permission to quote material on pages 111–112 and 211; to David Higham Associates for permission to quote the material on pages 172–3; and to the Society of Authors as the literary representative of the Estate of the late Philip Larkin to quote the material on pages 230 and 234.

My wife Belinda Kitchin has made all of this possible. I am not merely grateful to her, but much more, which has no place in an acknowledgements section of a book.

During the course of writing this book, my friend and literary agent Giles Gordon died in a tragic accident. He was a wonderful agent and a terrific person, vibrant and engaging, irreplaceable. Those of us who knew him felt enlarged by his presence, and his absence diminishes all our lives.

CONTENTS

CONTENTS

Introduction

I first saw them at a friend's, and it was love at first sight. It was 1969, I was twenty-four, an American post-graduate working on a DPhil in English. It was an exciting time, and I was in a state of high receptivity to the twin influences of Oxford life and the heady aura of the late sixties. But there was nothing psychedelic about my transforming moment, it was rather pedestrian really. On my friend's bookshelves, I noticed, next to the usual motley assortment of textbooks and used paperbacks, was a twenty-volume set of the Works of Charles Dickens, bound in brown cloth.

Even I could tell that it was an unprepossessing binding, drab and dusty. I have no idea why it had such an impact on me. I grew up in a bookish home, but we never had sets of books. We weren't that sort of family. Libraries had sets of books, not people. And there, in his tiny sitting room in an unassuming flat off the Iffley Road, was a set of Dickens! I was delighted by it, transfixed: a world of possibility opened before me. If he could have a set of Dickens, I could too. And why not Trollope? George Eliot? Swift? Johnson? And how grand they would look on my shelves, how . . . refined. I could build up a *library*, and not a mere assemblage of random, unassuming books. And in the evenings, I could sit in my library, and puff my pipe, and be a scholar. And a gentleman.

The very next morning I set off for our local Cowley Road bookshop, and got lucky. Not only did they have a twenty-volume set of Dickens, but it was lots better than my friend's, being bound in a delightful orange liberally adorned with gilt. I bought it for £10 ($18) (his had only cost £3 ($5.50)) and carried it home, where I gave it pride of place on my shelves and admired it greatly over the next few weeks, though I cannot recall ever opening any of the volumes, much less reading them.

But I had miscalculated badly. Christmas was coming up, and I had it in mind to buy my girlfriend one of those fashionable Afghan coats, covered in embroidery, smelling distinctly yakky. The only trouble was that they cost £30 ($55) (at the time I was living, quite comfortably, on £30 a *week*). And I'd blown my Christmas money on the Dickens. Casting my pretensions to gentlemanliness aside, I carted the books down to Blackwell's Antiquarian Department, and offered them for sale. To my astonishment, they offered £20 ($36). I had doubled my investment, in a few weeks. It was like a revelation. Surely, surely, if you could do this by accident, you could do it better on purpose?

Over the next year, I tried and tried. I bought obscure Victorian books with steel engravings – 'no market for *those*, sir' – and first editions by Charles Lever, and Radclyffe Hall, and John Masefield – '*quite* out of fashion, I'm afraid'. In the end, ironically, I did end up with a sort of library: books I had purchased in hope and kept in despair.

Gradually, I learned. After starting my lectureship in English at the University of Warwick, I continued to buy and sell the occasional book, supplementing my meagre salary. I had become a 'runner' – someone who buys books and sells them on to the trade. It was fun, with the delightful added attraction that it was a hobby that made money rather than cost it. By the middle of the 1980s I was making a few thousand pounds a year running books. A useful supplemental income, though hardly enough to live on. But I was sick of lecturing, and the confines and strictures of university life were uncongenial to me. Encouraged by both my wife and Mrs Thatcher (the former giving support, the latter a cheque for £27,000 ($49,000) redundancy pay) I quit, and decided to become a full-time rare book dealer, specializing in twentieth-century first editions and manuscripts. When I announced my (early) retirement, one of my colleagues slunk into my office, and confessed that he thought it 'very brave' of me to be leaving the department. I told him that, when I contemplated another twenty-five years as a university teacher, I thought it brave of him to stay. He wasn't amused.

Admittedly, it was a risky thing to do – we had two young children at the time – but it worked. I was happier being my own boss, swanning about buying and selling the odd book. In the first year I made twice my previous university salary, and had a hundred times more fun.

From the beginning, I was lucky. Whereas most rare book dealers acquire a large stock, mostly of books in the lower price ranges, I discovered – which rather surprised me – that what I was good at was dealing with expensive books. I don't know why this should be, why I can often see that a book priced at hundreds or thousands is *still* underpriced. It's a question of seeing an argument for extra value, and it has allowed me, over the years, access to a series of wonderful books.

In my business I have concentrated on acquiring the finest works by those modern writers whom I actually know about, and whom I used to teach: authors like Henry James, Conrad, T.S. Eliot, Joyce, Lawrence, Hemingway, Woolf, Beckett. Every year or so I issue a catalogue with a few nice things in it, maybe a hundred items, and eventually most of them sell, though more slowly than you would suppose.

It's an agreeable world, peopled by characters of all

sorts and persuasions, united only by their passion for collecting books. Because there's nothing as reassuring and reliable as a book. I don't mean physically, though books resist the passage of time considerably better than humans do, but emotionally. Books are good company, their presence brightens up a room: they become a defining feature of one's personal landscape. They are comforting because they are so stable. Unlike people, they don't change. At first reading a book may satisfy or disappoint, surprise or irritate, cause tears or laughter. But whatever happens is irrevocable: Little Nell will always die, James Bond will continue to defeat the forces of evil, Pooh will keep his paw in that honeypot.

As one gets older, and the enjoyment of reading is increasingly replaced by the pleasure of rereading, we become again like children, delighted by the constancy of the familiar. Yet in a lifetime spent with books, what has often fascinated me is how easily even the most famous of books could have been other than it is. Authors rewrite compulsively, and are never sure when a manuscript has found its final form. Editors and publishers, even friends, often have an immeasurable impact on the final form of a text. So a published book, frequently, is a collaborative effort, to which only the name of the author is eventually attached. Books have biographies, and the study of their geneses and later lives is frequently instructive.

A staggering number of books have been published – in England the figure is 110,000 a year – and most are soon, and justly, forgotten. But a very, very few works of literature become loved and celebrated, influence other writers, are used as texts in schools and universities, get translated into a host of languages. Because many such books were originally published in small numbers, collectors of literary first editions seek them out, and compete for the best copies. Unique examples are unearthed, in pristine condition, or with inscriptions or annotations by the author. Prices rise.

Tolkien's Gown traces the publishing history of twenty significant modern books, each of which is sought after by collectors of first editions. And, at this point, the biography of the book intersects with the biography of a rare book dealer. For each of us who has the fun and privilege to deal with great books has stories to tell: of where a rare book came from, and how, and where it ended up. And – which people always find compelling – how much money was involved.

This book began as a series of radio programmes on BBC Radio 4, entitled *Rare Books, Rare People,* and twelve of the chapters were originally aired there. These have, however, been substantially recast and rewritten for book publication. Fifteen minutes of radio time uses about 1,400 words, so each piece has been extended in length. The content has been altered as well. The radio series depended quite heavily on material from the BBC Sound Archive: marvellous recordings of Frieda Lawrence recalling how difficult her husband was, or Evelyn Waugh lambasting Joyce as 'gibberish', with a hard 'g'. Everyone loves hearing such snippets – imagine Frieda Lawrence having a voice! – and, in broadcasting, you learn to use such material for its own sake, rather than in the furtherance of an ongoing argument. So when it came time to transform the radio scripts into a format for reading, a lot of that audio material was unnecessary, and has been replaced with, I hope, more pertinent commentary.

I make no excuse for limiting *Tolkien's Gown* to modern books (if you will allow *The Picture of Dorian Gray* into that category). Twentieth-century literature is what I lectured in, what I deal in, and what I love. There is a certain arbitrariness in the choice of books. Though some of the classic texts of the modern period are included, many more are not. My choices have been dictated by several factors. First, I am interested in books with complex biographies. Second, they must be valued in the rare book market. Third, in many cases I have good stories to tell about them, from a dealer's point of view. It also helps when I like them, but that isn't necessary. Sometimes it's fun to write about a book you don't like.

I have arranged the chapters in a way which will, I hope, provide agreeable reading – as the author of a book of short stories or poems might do. Even this is rather hit or miss, and if any reader can discover method in it, I would be surprised.

Rick Gekoski

(rick@gekoski.com)

LOLITA

In my Catalogue Number 10, issued in the spring of 1988, as item 243, I offered the following book:

Nabokov, Vladimir. *Lolita*, London, 1959. First English edition, a presentation copy from Nabokov to his cousin Peter de Peterson and his wife, dated November 6, 1959, and with the author's characteristic little drawing of a butterfly beneath the inscription.

£3,250 ($5,900)

A few weeks later, I received a letter from Graham Greene, who was himself a book collector, and to whom I regularly sent my catalogues.

Dear Mr Gekoski,
If your copy of *Lolita*, which isn't even the true first edition, is worth £3,250, how much is the original Paris edition inscribed to me worth?
Yours sincerely,
Graham Greene

What a great book! The Olympia Press *Lolita* inscribed by Nabokov to Graham Greene! The book is an example of what rare book dealers call an 'association copy' – one presented by the author to someone of importance. In this case, Greene was not only important in himself, but he had played a crucial role in the publication of Nabokov's novel. The inscription to Greene added immensely to the book's value – an uninscribed copy, at the time, was worth about £200 ($360).

I wrote back immediately, in similarly minimalist style.

> Dear Mr Greene,
> More. Would you care to sell it?
>   Yours sincerely,
>   Rick Gekoski

In the (very) short correspondence that ensued Greene indicated that he might consider a sale, as he also had the first English edition inscribed to him, and didn't feel he needed both. I said that I would happily pay £4,000 ($7,200) for the Paris edition, and he agreed that he would bring it on his next visit to England.

In the event it wasn't until November that the meeting took place, in his room at the Ritz. As he opened the door, I was surprised by how tall he was, and by the expressiveness of his wet cornflower blue eyes. After we had drunk a quick vodka, he produced the *Lolita*:

published in two small dark green volumes, redolent of the Paris of the fifties. The inscription was breathtaking: 'For Graham Greene from Vladimir Nabokov, November 8, 1959', which was followed by a drawing of a large green butterfly, under which Nabokov had written 'green swallowtail dancing waisthigh'.

'It's fabulous,' I said, 'almost perfect.'

He raised his eyebrows, just a little. What was wrong with it?

'In a perfect world it would be inscribed in the year of publication [which was 1955], and it would be the first issue, instead of having the new price sticker on the rear cover.'

He nodded. He was known to be fond of bibliographic niceties.

'But it's terrific – real museum quality.'

'I'll talk,' he said.

'I'll give you £4,000.'

'You fail to understand me, Mr Gekoski. In the light of what you say I will take less.'

'On the contrary, Mr Greene, you fail to understand me. I won't pay less.'

He considered this for a moment.

'Would you like another vodka?' he asked.

We spent most of the next few hours talking about Conrad and Henry James. I think he began to take me seriously when I said that I thought that Henry James was funny, and couldn't understand why no one else did. He agreed wholeheartedly. We drank another vodka, in total critical harmony.

'I'm not in that league,' Greene said, with the conviction of someone who had thought a lot, reached the truth, and did not regret it. 'Conrad and James were Grade A novelists. I'm Grade B.' We had a final vodka in his honour: Grade B was pretty respectable, we reckoned.

He promised to keep in touch, which turned out to be more than a polite form of leave-taking. A few minutes later, I was decanted into Piccadilly by an obliging porter, clutching my *Lolita*, having made a new friend.

At nine the next morning the doorbell of my flat rang, and the pony-tailed, amiable figure of Elton John's lyricist, Bernie Taupin, peered in. Did I have anything in stock, he asked cautiously (I was in a bathrobe, ingesting aspirins), that his wife might buy him for a Christmas present?

However bad your hangover, you don't send Bernie Taupin away, much less his chequebook-clutching wife. Well, I admitted rashly, I did just buy something rather nice . . .

It was more than nice, it was irresistible: Bernie was both a Greene collector and a *Lolita*-admirer. Once he had his hands on the book, it was clear he was never going to let go of it. I'd made a mistake, and I realized it immediately. Never sell a great book too quickly:

you need time to do a little research, have a think, get the price to the right level.

'How much is it?' asked the willing Mrs T, seeing the bibliophilic lovelight gleaming in her husband's eye.

'Nine thousand pounds,' I said, hoping this might put her off.

She didn't even blink, or ask for a discount. Five minutes later, I had a cheque, a headache, and an appalling sense of regret. I wasn't sure if I had under-sold the book – £9,000 ($16,200) was a lot of money in those days – but I was certain I had under-owned it. You like to savour a wonderful book, have it near you for a while, until the magic begins to wear off, and commercial imperatives reassert themselves. Alas, poor *Lolita*, I hardly knew her.

Lolita was first published by Maurice Girodias in Paris in 1955. Girodias, who described himself as 'a second-generation Anglo-French pornographer', was the son of Manchester-born Jack Kahane, whose Obelisk Press had published Henry Miller's *Tropic of Cancer* in the 1930s. Girodias founded the Olympia Press in 1953 and was committed, like his father, to publishing good quality, sexually explicit literature in English. Some of his authors were writers of the highest quality – Samuel Beckett, William Burroughs, Henry Miller, Jean Genet, J.P. Donleavy – while others (often writing under pseu-donyms) were straightforward purveyors of what

5

Girodias termed DBs (dirty books). These were usually issued under different imprints, one of which was puckishly entitled the Traveller's Companion Series. But even his pornographic books (*The Enormous Bed, Rape, How To Do It, With Open Mouth*) were literate and well written. Many were ghosted by such well-known writers as Christopher Logue and Alex Trocchi, who were always happy to make a few francs while having fun.

At this time Vladimir Nabokov, with a couple of respectfully reviewed books out in America, was a relatively obscure figure, quietly but brilliantly lecturing at Cornell University. He was anxiously seeking a publisher for his new book: 'the enormous, mysterious, heartbreaking novel that, after five years of monstrous misgivings and diabolical labours, I have more or less completed. It has no precedent in literature.'

But *Lolita* had been turned down by five successive American publishers. Though *The Partisan Review* had agreed to publish an excerpt, it stipulated that it must appear under the author's own name – which Nabokov, worried that a naïve American public would identify the first-person narrator with himself, declined to allow.

Prospective publishers thought *Lolita,* however much they admired it, a dangerous book. Its middle-aged hero, Humbert Humbert, is sexually besotted with a twelve-year-old girl. Lolita is certainly not the adolescent nymphet portrayed by Sue Lyon in Stanley Kubrick's 1962 film. She weighs five and a half stone, has measurements of 27–23–29: palpably still a child. The novel was doubly shocking: not only was it a sympathetic rendering of the inward world of a paedophile, but the object of his affections is a sexually aware, provocative little girl. It is not wholly surprising, in the repressive atmosphere of the 1950s, that one prospective American publisher recommended that it 'be buried under a stone for a thousand years'.

It is continually surprising to me that Nabokov got away with it so comprehensively, but if you look at the opening paragraphs, you get some idea of how:

> Lolita, light of my life, fire of my loins. My sin, my soul. Lo-lee-ta: the tip of the tongue taking a trip of three steps down the palate to tap, at three, on the teeth. Lo. Lee. Ta.
>
> She was Lo, plain Lo, in the morning, standing four feet ten in one sock. She was Lola in slacks. She was Dolly at school. She was Dolores on the dotted line. But in my arms she was always Lolita.

This faces the issue squarely enough, but the playfully sensuous elegance of the language is enough to make the most hardened paedophile detumesce. Whatever this is going to be, the opening announces, and whatever disapproval it may engender, this is not your usual DB.

Indeed, several readers of the resulting edition demanded their money back. This wasn't up to the usual Olympian standard, they complained. You could hardly even understand it, as if it were written in a foreign language. Which, of course, it was. English was for Nabokov, as it had been for Conrad, not a second, but a third language. (Refined Europeans of the period usually had French as their second language.) Nabokov's first publications, dating from the early 1920s, were in Russian, and were followed by several books in French. It wasn't until 1941 that he published his first book (*The Real Life of Sebastian Knight*) in English. His English, again like that of Conrad, was suffused by a sense of discovery and delight in the linguistic possibilities of a new tongue. It was sensuous, arcane, both idiomatic and formal, roiling with breathtaking and unexpected constructions. It sounded fabulously new, freshly invented, and it is all too easy to imagine it spoken in a Russian accent.

Failing to find an American publisher with the nerve to take on the book, Nabokov was advised to send the manuscript to Girodias at the Olympia Press. It was an unlikely choice, based on a combination of ignorance and expediency, and was almost certain to end in tears.

Girodias was something of a rogue, a cosmopolitan bon viveur who made up each year's prospective publishing list by inventing a bunch of steamy titles, issuing a prospectus for them, and then desperately trying to find someone to write them once the orders came flooding in. Nabokov, by way of the most extreme contrast, was a highly refined Russian aristocrat, committed only to the highest forms of literature.

But Girodias had a great eye, loved *Lolita*, and agreed at once to publish:

. . . the story was a rather magical demonstration of something I had so often dreamed about but never found: the treatment of one of the major human passions in a manner both completely sincere and absolutely legitimate. I sensed that *Lolita* would become the one great modern work of art to demonstrate once and for all the futility of moral censorship.

Knowing that Girodias was notorious as a publisher of sexually explicit work, Nabokov wrote to him with some concern: 'You and I know *Lolita* is a serious work with a serious purpose. I hope the public will accept it as such. A *succès de scandale* would distress me.'

But *succès de scandale* is just what he got, and it was the best thing that could have happened to him. If the naïve college professor thought that the publication of such a book might be met with universal admiration, Girodias certainly did not. He liked a fuss: it was good for sales.

When Graham Greene chose *Lolita* as one of his three best books of the year, in the 1955 Christmas issue of the *Sunday Times*, it brought a hitherto obscure novel to the notice of the English reading public. But the book rocketed into notoriety when John Gordon, the editor of the *Sunday Express*, attacked it in response to Greene's praise:

> Without doubt it is the filthiest book I have ever read. Sheer unrestrained pornography. Its central character is a pervert with a passion for debauching what he calls 'nymphets', girls aged from 11 to 14. The entire book is devoted to an exhaustive, uninhibited, and entirely disgusting description of his pursuits and successes.

Greene responded by forming the John Gordon Society – members included Christopher Isherwood, Angus Wilson, and A.J. Ayer – which was dedicated to examining and condemning 'all offensive books, plays, paintings, sculptures and ceramics'. An immediate campaign was begun to make sure nobody used dirty words in games of Scrabble.

Though pleased by the burgeoning sales, Nabokov was a little chagrined by the furore: 'My poor *Lolita* is having a rough time. The pity is that if I had made her a boy, or a cow, or a bicycle, Philistines might never have flinched.'

He had been sufficiently anxious about his position at Cornell to wish to publish the novel under a pseudonym, but Girodias had eventually talked him round. If the novel ever had to be defended in court, appeals to its literary merits would certainly be undermined if its author wouldn't own up to it.

American publishers soon renewed their interest in the book, noting how many copies of the Olympia edition were being imported into America, unprosecuted by the vigilant moral guardians in US Customs. Greene was actively hoping to get it published in England. Soon enough, Nabokov no longer needed Girodias, whose lax business practices he found increasingly infuriating. The contract they had agreed gave Girodias a generous one-third of any future English language and translation rights, which were likely to add up to a lot of money. Nabokov tried to find a way to break the contract, but couldn't.

After some negotiation, Girodias agreed to a smaller percentage, and Putnams published the book in America. It sold over 100,000 copies in the first three weeks, the hottest bestseller since *Gone With the Wind*. There was some reaction. The town of Lolita, Texas changed its name to Jackson, and Groucho Marx declared he would wait six years to read it, until Lolita was eighteen. But most reviewers admired the novel for the masterpiece it certainly is: an engrossing mix of tragedy and comedy, opulently well written. The following year it was published in London by Weidenfeld & Nicolson, on 8 November 1959.

So it turns out that the date on the inscribed Olympia Press *Lolita* that I bought from Graham Greene was publication day of the English edition – a fact that I discovered somewhat later. But when a copy of the Weidenfeld & Nicolson *Lolita* turned up at Sotheby's two years ago, inscribed on the same date, I seemed to be the only person in the rooms who recognized its significance. I bought it relatively cheaply and sold it relatively well. As for the original copy that I purchased from Graham Greene, I bought it back in 1992 for £13,000 ($23,500), and soon sold it on to a collector in New York. He got a bargain. When the book reappeared at a Christie's sale in 2002, it fetched the astounding price of $264,000. I was sitting in the rooms at the time, feeling astonished, and sick with seller's remorse.

Still, I've done pretty well out of *Lolita*, though not as well as Nabokov or Girodias. On the proceeds, Nabokov was able to retire from his teaching position, to devote himself to writing and butterfly collecting. Girodias, suddenly rich from this unexpected windfall, opened two Parisian night-clubs, a restaurant, three bars, and a theatre. Five years later he went bankrupt.

THE HOBBIT

In 1966, in my first year as a post-graduate at Merton College, Oxford, I occupied a small college room at 21 Merton Street. It was spare but romantic – there were views of Magdalen Tower, the bells of which kept me awake all night – and exceedingly cold. I outraged my college scout, Charley Carr, by keeping my two-bar heater on all night, at a cost of almost £4 ($7) for the whole term. Over-heating, he informed me, was both expensive and bad for you.

He would never have accused me of being a spoiled, rich American, which, by the standards of the time, I was. Charley was far too polite for that; not merely polite, but kindly and sensitive. Though he had played both football and cricket for Oxfordshire, and could hold his own in men's company, he had a fine and delicate nature that was uncompromised by what many would have regarded as a position of subservience. For a scout, as Charley recognized, was not a servant but an employee of the college, whose remit was to keep a paternal eye on the students in his house: to make sure they were tidy, and comfortable, and behaved themselves.

Early in 1972, after I took my DPhil and moved up to Warwick to teach at the new university, I got a phone call from Charley. Mr Tolkien, he informed me, had moved into 21 Merton Street, and asked him to help clear away a lot of unwanted rubbish.

'You liked Mr Tolkien's books, didn't you?' he asked.

'Very much,' I said hopefully.

'Well,' said Charley, 'he's asked me to throw out his old college gown, and I was thinking maybe old Rick would want it.'

At first it was a disappointment. I'd envisaged a chunk of his library, but when I thought about it, I did want the gown. Why not? Shades of Gandalf, right? On examination the raggedy old scrap of black cloth had a name-tag sewn into it: 'R. Tolkien'. What better sign of provenance could you ask for? I declined the further offer of several pairs of Mr Tolkien's shoes, and a few tired tweed jackets. Gratefully, I bundled the gown into a plastic bag, had a few beers with Charley, and carried my Precious (as Gollum would call it) triumphantly home to Warwickshire. Where it sat, totally forgotten in our attic, for some ten years.

Early in 1982, dissatisfied with university life and increasingly engaged by my new vocation as a book scout, I decided to issue my first catalogue of books for sale. I'd assembled a number of good things in my personal collection of first editions, but had soon tired of them. It was more fun to buy and sell books than to keep them. That way you kept acquiring interesting things, could suck the pleasure out of them, sell them, and move on to something new.

My Catalogue Number 1 was issued in the autumn of 1982, in green paper covers which listed, inside a ruled box, the highlights contained within. I thought the total effect was elegant, until my printer handed me his bill, and looked at the catalogue fondly. 'Cheap and cheerful!' he said. 'That's the way to do it!'

The catalogue sold very well, because the books, which had been assembled over the previous six years, were reasonably priced. 'That's easy!' said one member of the book trade dismissively. 'But can you do it again? Can you do it every six months?'

I was anxious to convince my new customers that I was the sort of dealer who found unusual things. Books were easy, everybody had those. And so, as item 197 of Catalogue Number 2, issued six months later, I included Mr Tolkien's gown. My description of its condition now seems a little over-arch: 'original black cloth, slightly frayed and with a little soiling, spine sound'. An added attraction, not evident in those innocent times, was that from one of its many DNA-rich stains one might eventually hope to clone a small army of Tolkiens, and fill a senior common room full of professors brandishing epics. I priced the gown, somewhat arbitrarily, at £550 ($1,000), and it sold to an eccentric academic from the American South, who claimed he was going to wear it at his university's yearly commencement exercise. Charley was astonished, and used the windfall to go to Cornwall for a fortnight.

Not very much later I had a call from the young novelist Julian Barnes, who was himself a book collector, though I believe he has since abandoned the habit. He'd had my catalogue, he said, and was interested in item 197.

'It's sold, I'm afraid.'

He snorted.

'I didn't say I wanted to buy it. I said I was interested in it.'

'OK . . .'

'It got me thinking about writers' clothes, and the market in them. How much would you pay me for, say, James Joyce's smoking jacket?'

'Did he have one?'

'Let's assume he had,' he said, in a markedly patrician tone.

'I don't know,' I said warily, uncertain where this was going. Joyce's smoking jacket sounded rather enticing. Where would Julian Barnes have got hold of it? Did it have provenance? How much would he take for it?

'Or,' Julian continued relentlessly, 'what about D.H. Lawrence's underpants? Or Gertrude Stein's bra?'

'I don't know,' I said, belatedly catching on. 'I presume they're from your own collection? Do you wear them yourself?'

'You see the point. Where do you draw the line?' he asked, as if we were petting in the back of a car.

A few days later, his article appeared – was it in the *TLS*? – having some fun with the idea of trading in writers' garments. It made me relieved I hadn't catalogued a pair of Mr Tolkien's shoes as well. I don't believe I have sold any writers' clothes since, though I did once catalogue the first cutting of Sylvia Plath's hair, done when she was two years old. And I still fantasize, a little, about Joyce's smoking jacket.

When Tolkien moved into the equally austere rooms directly below mine, he found a quiet place in which to finish both his life and *The Silmarillion*. He was rich by then, and could have found something much more comfortable, but he loved returning to college life. He was a decent, shambling old chap, an unlit pipe in his mouth, his eyes focused inward, so that you never felt he was actually addressing you. Presumably he was internally somewhere in his fictional Middle Earth, lost in epic musings. 'Morning,' he'd say vaguely as he passed, as if he were asking the time of day, or guessing what it was.

Tolkien was as near to a celebrity, in the modern

sense, as Merton had ever produced. Sir Thomas Bodley was a Mertonian, and so were Max Beerbohm and T.S. Eliot, but none of them received sacks of fan mail, or crowds of autograph-seekers. At weekends a small throng of colourful, hairy creatures would coagulate and gawp outside 21 Merton Street, looking like extras from the film of *The Lord of the Rings*.

The world had gone Tolkien mad. *The Lord of the Rings* trilogy had been completed, to great acclaim, in 1955, but it had, as it were, been reinvented in the sixties, when the first American paperbacks were issued. Everyone I knew had read it. It was enchanting: an unexpected combination of sublimity, erudition and whimsy that meshed perfectly with the spirit of the times. It was terrific to read if you were stoned and, improbably enough, Tolkien joined the Beatles, Andy Warhol and Timothy Leary as a star in the psyche-delic galaxy. American students wore 'Gandalf for President' badges, a Vietnamese dancer in Saigon was spotted with the eye of Sauron on his shield, in Borneo a Frodo Society was created. By 1968, world-wide sales had passed three million copies. Tolkien was more than a little bemused by the fuss, referring ironically to 'my deplorable cultus', though he rather liked making so much money.

The books sold everywhere, and to everyone. They were adored by children, partly because they were not written specifically for them. They weren't easy:

the vocabulary could be abstruse, the plot lines complex, the genealogies obscure. You had to concentrate. Each book was written, Tolkien insisted, 'for itself'. In a lecture on Fairy Stories presented at St Andrews University, Tolkien maintained that he never wrote 'for children', as if that were in itself patronizing. 'Children are not a class or kind, they are a heterogeneous collection of immature persons,' he wrote, which presumably was not intended to sound patronizing.

If his stories appeared 'childish', he insisted, that was because *he* was. I was too. I'd read, and reread, the trilogy, then went backwards in time and read *The Hobbit*, which had been published in 1937. It was simpler, more obviously aimed at children, which Tolkien later considered a fault, but equally charming. I wouldn't wish to reread any of the books today. I suspect they'd seem arch, and a bit snobbish, mannered and pedantic. I enjoyed a lot of things then that would now seem a little jejune. But what I really regret is not that I read Tolkien's books with such enthusiasm, but that I didn't get him to inscribe them for me.

At the time, you could still get first editions of the *Lord of the Rings* trilogy for some reasonable multiple of their original published prices, while a *Hobbit* in its dustwrapper might have set you back £50 ($90). I knew very little about first editions at the time, and if you had told me I would spend a good part of my adult life dealing in them, I would have been astonished, and horrified. Who cared about what edition you read? It was content that mattered.

It was curious that Tolkien should have ended his writing life with *The Silmarillion* because that was where it began. He was, in both his academic and fictional work, an endless tinkerer and reviser, who would rather put something aside than publish it in less than perfect state. The final book, a dark and ambitious saga, had been conceived in the 1920s, and had partly sprung – as did all his work – from stories that he told his young children. When he put it aside, he began telling the children – during what they called their 'Winter Reads' – the long story that was to become *The Hobbit.*

Tolkien described the genesis of hobbits as if they were *objets trouvés,* thrown up on the shore of his unconscious. During the course of grading some examination scripts, early in the 1930s, Tolkien discovered that one of the candidates had left a page entirely blank. On it, he remembered:

I wrote . . . 'In a hole in the ground there lived a hobbit.' Names always generate a story in my mind. Eventually I thought I'd better find out what hobbits were like.

What they were like, he later reflected, was himself:

> I am in fact a hobbit in all but size. I like gardens, trees, and unmechanised farmlands; I smoke a pipe, and like good plain food (unrefridgerised) . . . I like, and even dare to wear in these dull days, ornamental waistcoats. I am fond of mushrooms (out of a field); have a very simple sense of humour; I go to bed late and get up late (when possible). I do not travel very much.

Generically, hobbits were simple, rustic Englishmen (though shorter and with hairy feet), of limited imaginative range in their daily lives, but capable, when moved, of great courage and resourcefulness.

But to admit that *l'hobbit c'est moi* is not to deny the myriad influences of Tolkien's reading. He was at pains, in a letter to the editor of the *Observer* in 1938, to deny that his hobbits were based on the furry little African men described by Julian Huxley. Rather, he admitted, his major source was *Beowulf*, supplemented with dwarf and wizard names from the *Elder Edda*. By implication, *The Hobbit* was the sort of book any imaginative and self-respecting student of Anglo Saxon might have written.

Tolkien began typing the story in the first years of the 1930s, but typically did not feel able to finish it. Various friends, and particularly C.S. Lewis, understood that he was a painstaking writer, read the manuscript and encouraged him to get on with it. But it might well have continued unregarded, had not one of his post-graduate students recommended that he send it to the publishers, Allen and Unwin.

Unwin, unsure what to make of the submission, offered the manuscript to his ten-year-old son Rayner, and asked him for a reader's report (for which he was promised a shilling). Rayner liked it:

> Bilbo Baggins was a hobbit who lived in his hobbit-hole and *never* went for adventures. At last Gandalf the wizard and his dwarves perswaded him to go. He had a very exciting time fighting goblins and wargs. At last they got to the lonley [sic] mountain; Smaug, the dragon who gawreds it is killed, and after a terrific battle with the goblins he returned home – rich! This book, with the help of maps, does not need any illustrations it is good and should appeal to children between the ages of 5 and 9.

Rayner's father disagreed on only one point and commissioned Tolkien, who was a talented amateur artist, to provide a design for the dustwrapper. Tolkien was modest about his abilities, observing only that 'the pictures seem to me mostly only to prove that the author cannot draw'. Yet his perfect dustwrapper illustration continues to adorn the book, and adds considerably to its charm, not to mention its value on a first edition. Coloured in blue, green and black it depicts a forest in the foreground with snow-capped mountains behind, and a blue and white sky in which dragons are swooping. On the borders are Tolkien's runic letters, which have a magical air and spell out the full title of the book: 'The Hobbit, Or There and Back Again, being the record of a year's journey made by Bilbo Baggins; compiled from his memoirs by J.R.R. Tolkien and published by George Allen and Unwin.'

The book was published in September of 1937, in an edition of 1,500 copies, and reprinted within a few months. By Christmas season, the demand for copies was such that (the publishers reported breathlessly) 'the crisis was so acute that we fetched part of the reprint from our printers at Woking in a private car.'

'It sounds quite exciting,' Tolkien replied, delighted at the sales and favourable reviews. *The Hobbit* has never been out of print since. It is one of the most sought after of all children's books, and decent copies preserving the superb dustwrapper can now fetch £30,000 ($54,000).

Oh, the follies of youth! By the time that I met him, so great were the demands of strangers that Tolkien would only sign books for friends, or for Merton men. It would have been so easy, and if I had kept the inscribed copies they would provide the basis for a comfortable old age. Over the last decade Tolkien prices have risen astonishingly – faster than the NASDAQ index – first in anticipation of the film version of *The Lord of the Rings*, and latterly in response to it.

An inscribed *Hobbit*? Perhaps £75,000 ($135,000). An inscribed *Lord of the Rings*? About £50,000 ($90,000). Mind you, I've never sold a book inscribed to me, so I guess I would leave them to my children. But I would sell, if the need were sufficient and a bibliophilic wolf came to the door. Wolves eat books, and they're particularly keen on Tolkiens.

LORD OF THE FLIES

I have a friend who is a book collector and lawyer, a shrewd judge of a book, and an even keener one of possible cause for litigation. And from the tone of his voice over the phone, the conjunction of the two was exciting him terribly.

'You've got him,' he said. 'It's an easy case! I'd even take it for free. We'll screw the bastard!'

It was 1985, and he had just finished reading William Golding's new novel, *The Paper Men*, which has as its protagonist a testy, Golding-like novelist who is hounded by its anti-hero, a large, bearded American academic, one Rick L. Turner. This 'Rick' wishes to become the Golding-figure's biographer, and is (among other things) discovered by the novelist rooting around in his rubbish bins, in the hope of carrying away some significant biographical data.

'It's libellous, no doubt about it! Just say the word!' And, in my friend's view, the case against Golding became even stronger when I informed him that the name of the pesty American biographer had been changed from 'Jake' at proof stage to 'Rick' in the published volume, presumably in response to his increasing irritation at my recent bibliographical intrusion in his life. I'd seen the proof, and read the book, so none of this came as news to me. I had already decided on my attitude to it. Sadly, but demonstrably, winners of the Nobel Prize for Literature have ignored me pretty comprehensively. Not a word in Boris Pasternak, or Octavio Paz, or even Saul Bellow. So if a Nobel Laureate decided I was welcome in the corpus of his works, even a parody seemed to me better than nothing. I'm not all that proud.

During this time, I had been working with a somewhat resistant and truculent Golding on a bibliography of his works. He had consented unwillingly to the project – 'It will be like drinking my own bathwater,' he said – adding that it made him 'feel posthumous'. (By the time the book was published, in 1994, he was.) Though he had maintained that he would neither help nor hinder the project, he eventually, almost gracefully, allowed me occasional visits to his house outside Truro to examine his papers and copies of his own books.

It was never a comfortable experience, and he felt symbolically violated by it. Once, when I asked if I might examine some papers relating to his early publications, he answered testily, and suggestively: 'I'm not letting anyone into *my* drawers!' His was a nice example of that aggression perfected by diffident prep school masters, at once unassuming and supremely arrogant. He was shy, and only at ease with family and friends, or after a couple of drinks.

On the advice of Golding's editor, Charles Monteith, I always brought a couple of bottles of Puligny Montrachet to the Goldings, which we would drink over lunch. One afternoon, having consumed a respectable amount of the wine, Bill (as he liked to be called) shuffled off to bang away at his piano, while I worked in his study. He was an enthusiastic, rather than a skilled pianist, and he could make an impressive racket. Doing bibliographic research is achingly dull and requires discipline, and the infernal clamour was pretty awful. All of a sudden there was silence, and Bill lurched through the door.

'What's it for?' he asked aggressively. 'Who gives a damn about it?'

'Well,' I said judiciously, trying to decide which was worse, the noise or the interrogation. 'It will be useful to anyone who wants to know the scope of your work, what you've written, and when.'

'Why don't they just read the damn books?'

'They may not know what you have written, or when, or who it was published by.'

He looked doubtful. Presumably that wasn't the sort of reader he wanted anyway.

'Or suppose someone wanted to know which ones have been translated into, say, Bulgarian? A bibliography would help them no end.'

He looked at me scathingly, and withdrew. Bang, crash, wallop came the sound of what I thought might be some sort of mazurka, which sounded like a challenge.

The next morning, though, came a special treat. I was invited to accompany him down to his bank branch in Truro, to inspect – with an eye to valuation – the holograph manuscript of *Lord of the Flies*. As we entered the bank, a slight hush enveloped the tellers, as Golding was clearly their greatest local celebrity. In fact, on his first visit to the bank after being awarded his knighthood in 1988, a tongue-tied young woman teller had blushed bright red, and stuttered, 'Good morning, Sir Golding,' which made him feel, he confessed, like a character out of Malory.

The manuscript, which was kept in a safe deposit box, was a remarkably homely object. He had used school exercise books to write in, often huddled over coffee in a corner of the staff room during breaks. What was most striking was the fluency of the writing – there were very few amendments or corrections, and he was later to recall that he had the story so clear in his mind that he felt he was copying, rather than composing it.

I was rather surprised that he would consider

selling it, but he was tormented, in his later years, by anxiety about money. So acute was this that Lady Golding begged me, one evening, to reason with him about it.

'It's all right for you,' he remarked grumpily, 'you're a rich man.'

I offered, sight unseen, to swap financial positions with him, before suggesting to him that his worries were symbolic. 'What's it *really* about?' I asked: 'loss of power or control? Declining hold on things? It's quite common to feel that way at your time of life.'

He glared at my impertinence. 'Don't be so bloody stupid,' he said, 'it's about *money*.'

His financial concerns were, he admitted, exacerbated by the terror that he might go to jail for tax evasion.

'I have nightmares about it,' he said.

'Talk to Rick about it,' urged Ann. 'He'll tell you how silly it all is.'

'In 1961,' Golding said, 'I visited Canada, and did a series of lectures. Well, one of the universities gave me a cheque for $100.' He paused, distressed at having to remember and speak of it.

'And?'

'I cashed it in Canada, and spent it.'

'And?'

'That's all.'

'It never happened again?'

29

He shuddered. 'Certainly not! I lie awake at night worrying that Inland Revenue will catch up with me, and put me in jail.'

I was careful not to laugh. 'Well,' I said judiciously, 'I don't suppose you find that many Nobel Prize winners in jail for tax evasion.'

'Lester Piggott was sent to jail!'

'He was a jockey, and it was for a VAT fraud,' I said. 'The figure was apparently four million pounds.'

'The principle is the same,' said Bill, with conviction.

So he had come, I think, to regard the manuscript of *Lord of the Flies* as a little nest egg, and was receptive to the idea of cashing it in. He was a man of many doubts, but he had never doubted, from the moment of its inception, the value of *Lord of the Flies*, as either text or object. When he finished the first draft, he announced to his family that one day it would 'win him the Nobel Prize'. And, though the prize is given for lifetime achievement and not for a single work, he was right.

He also had little doubt as to its exact financial value. Though he had asked me to value it, he had a figure in mind.

'If you can find a nice rich American or Japanese,' he said, with an attempt at worldly offhandedness utterly foreign to his nature, 'I would take a million for it.'

'A million what?' I asked, maybe a little puckishly.

He seemed to consider.

'Pounds, of course!' (As if I had insulted the Queen.)

'But Bill,' I said, as reasonably as I could, 'the only twentieth-century manuscript to have fetched anything remotely like that sort of figure is Kafka's *The Trial*.'

He nodded his head, as if this confirmed his view.

'Anyway,' I said, 'there is no buyer out there at that sort of price.'

'Surely there's got to be some super-rich collector who would be dying to have it!'

'In my experience you don't get to be super-rich by not caring what you pay for things. Value for money is the only way the rich can protect themselves.'

He glared at me. Clearly I was a rotten dealer.

'Get me a million,' he said, 'and you can have 5 per cent.'

Before the war, Bill Golding was a young schoolteacher at Bishop Wordsworth School in Salisbury. He joined the Royal Navy in 1940, and returned to work, six years later:

There was a time when I would have said we are not evil, and by the time I had found out after the Second World War what men had done to each other, what men had done to their own people, really then I was forced to postulate something which I could not see coming out of normal human

31

nature as portrayed in good books and all the rest of it, I thought there must be some kind of principle of evil at work.

He was trained as a scientist, and, on his return to teaching, he became fascinated by his pupils. Who were they? What were they capable of? He'd never thought about them properly before. If men were capable of evil on a grand scale, as he had learned, how did this affect his view of boys? His pupils didn't know it at the time, but his horror at man's inhumanity to man was slowly transforming itself into a new but related interest: boys' inhumanity to boy.

Lord of the Flies was written about schoolboys, and at school, and at speed. But it's one thing to have a manuscript, quite another to get someone to publish it. It has been suggested that *Lord of the Flies* was rejected by twenty-two consecutive publishers. I don't believe it for a minute; only an idiot would choose Faber and Faber as their twenty-third choice. But there's no question that the dog-eared manuscript, with its plaintive covering letter, certainly made the rounds: 'I am writing a novel about a group of boys who get dumped on a desert island and about the innate wound in human nature that makes them evolve an unsatisfactory type of society, would this interest you?'

Unsurprisingly, this lumpy précis didn't interest Jonathan Cape, André Deutsch, Fred Warburg or

Victor Gollancz. In September of 1953 Golding sent the manuscript to Faber and Faber, where it almost fell at the first hurdle. Charles Monteith, then a young editor at Faber's, recalled the moment:

Every Tuesday morning, a professional reading lady came and we'll call her Miss Parkinson (it's not her real name) and Miss Parkinson was a terrifying figure to us because she was very, very professional indeed and she read for a number of publishers. She was said to have an eagle eye, incredible shrewdness, and she also had a great gift for summing up a book in a telling phrase, which she then wrote on the author's covering letter which was attached to the front of the manuscript. Miss Parkinson had looked through it and she wrote a terse comment at the top which said 'Time: The Future. Absurd and uninteresting fantasy about the explosion of an atomic bomb on the colonies and a group of children who land in jungle country near New Guinea. Rubbish and dull. Pointless.'

Undeterred, Monteith had a look at the despised submission, and thought it had promise. It began badly – with a twelve page account of a nuclear explosion – but picked up after that. Monteith recommended that his colleagues have a look at it. The Sales Director was unconvinced, and regarded the text as unpublishable.

But Geoffrey Faber, encouraging his young editor, suggested that Monteith (without making any commitment to publishing) talk to the author and see if together they could bang it into some sort of shape.

'I thought he was probably a young clergyman because of the obvious and strong theological skeleton to the book. It's frightfully obvious now that I should have guessed he was a school master.' Golding was no prima donna. He was anxious to hear criticism, and quite willing to rewrite. Monteith's major suggestion was that the boys be deposited directly on the island, and the first twelve pages excised.

But even after Golding and Monteith had agreed upon a text, they were at odds over the title. *Strangers From Within*, as it was then called, didn't exactly trip off the tongue. What should replace it? Golding had a few ideas, each of them worse than the previous: *A Cry of Children*? *Nightmare Island*? *To Find an Island*? Desperately, Monteith went back to *The Tempest*, trying to find a title about an island there. But it was eventually his colleague at Faber, Alan Pringle, who suggested *Lord of the Flies*. The idea was an immediate hit.

Almost exactly a year after it was first submitted to Faber and Faber, *Lord of the Flies* was published, in September of 1954. The firm submitted the book to the Cheltenham Festival First Novel Competition, but it failed even to make the shortlist. Slowly, though, the

34

novel began to attract good reviews. There was a particularly enthusiastic one from Stevie Smith, who called it 'beautiful and desperate. Something quite out of the ordinary.' But the sales only took off when E.M. Forster selected it as his book of the year for 1954. He was later to say of *Lord of the Flies* that:

> it may help a few grown-ups to be less complacent and more compassionate, to support Ralph, respect Piggy, control Jack, and lighten a little the darkness of man's heart. At the present moment, if I may speak personally it is respect for Piggy that seems needed most. I do not find it in our leaders.

That was written in 1962, but it seems as true today as it seemed then. In the intervening period, *Lord of the Flies* has been translated into at least thirty-three different languages and sold some twenty million copies. A nice crisp first edition in dustwrapper is now worth £5,000 ($9,000).

I'm not at all clear what the manuscript is worth. Manuscripts are harder to value than books, and one usually has to do it by analogy, either with other manuscripts by the same author, or manuscripts of similar importance. *Lord of the Flies* is thus a special case, because very few post-war novels are as important and famous. One thinks of the manuscripts of *Catcher in the Rye* and *Catch-22*, either of which would fetch a very large price, but neither of which has come on the market.

When Golding asked me for a valuation, all those years ago, I took advice from a number of leading dealers, whose estimates of its value ranged from £50,000 to £250,000 ($90,000 to $450,000). I conveyed this information to him gingerly, and he snorted with contempt. Nobody was getting into that drawer so cheaply. I suppose the latter figure is now closer to the mark, if you could find a rich American or Japanese. After all, the manuscript of *On The Road* recently fetched over two million dollars, because that novel had a special place in the heart of at least one rich American. Who knows? Maybe *Lord of the Flies* does too.

THE PICTURE OF
DORIAN GRAY

In the popular imagination, literary lunches or dinners have a fabled allure, especially to that large body of readers that doesn't attend them. Though frequently dull, and most often unproductive, they conjure up images of bibulous evenings at the Groucho Club and sparkling repartee at the Garrick. Most curious readers love stories about their favourite authors at play, and it is true that many of the memorable quips and sallies of literary history have been delivered over food and (particularly) drink. But unless the oysters are mortally off, or the scene is set in an Agatha Christie novel, literary dinners rarely terminate in death.

I do not think it entirely frivolous, however, to maintain that the events on the evening of 30 August 1889, when the publisher J.M. Stoddard dined with two promising young authors, led directly to the chain of events – fascinating in their tragic inexorability – that culminated in the death in Paris, some eleven years later, of Oscar Wilde.

Mr Stoddard was trawling London in search of new fiction for the American *Lippincott's Monthly Magazine*, and had invited Mr Wilde and Dr Arthur Conan Doyle to join him for dinner. The young Irishman had made a spectacular impression during his American lecture tour in 1882, when the lily-toting chatterbox had proclaimed himself an apostle of art for art's sake. As a personality he was an immense hit, though it was hard to find anyone who had read anything he had written.

Wilde's literary production, even by the time of his dinner with Stoddard, was relatively slight: he had published a few short stories in magazines, two limited editions of surprisingly inert plays, a florid and unmemorable book of verse, and a perfect children's book, *The Happy Prince*. For some years, he had lived off the brilliance of his undergraduate performances, his wit and charm, but was in some danger, at the age of thirty-five, of falling into the suspended animation of the perpetually promising. If he was the genius he had proclaimed himself to be on entering America in 1882, it was about time he produced the works to prove it.

Both of the young writers responded to Mr Stoddard's blandishments: Conan Doyle produced the second of the Sherlock Holmes volumes, *The Sign of*

Four, and Wilde (after a false start) came up with *The Picture of Dorian Gray* – an exceptional haul for a night's work on the publisher's part. Wilde was paid £200 ($360) for the serial rights, and completed the book in only a few months.

Though *Dorian Gray* was the result of that famous dinner, it had its imaginative genesis in an event in 1887, when Wilde had his portrait painted by the Canadian, Frances Richards. Gazing with pleasure upon the finished image, Wilde remarked sadly: 'What a tragic thing it is . . . this portrait will never grow older, and I shall. If it was only the other way.' The only other way was, of course, through art, which was never for Wilde to be confused with life, because infinitely preferable to it.

In the ensuing novel, Dorian Gray's portrait slowly reveals the ravages of time upon its subject, while the exquisite corporeal Dorian is apparently exempt from them. Fascinated by this increasing disparity between his body and soul, he becomes obsessed by the tell-tale ugliness of his image, while continuing to lead the dissolute life that causes its gradual corruption. When, in his final fit of madness, he stabs his portrait with a knife, it is himself he kills. His servants discover a corpse almost unrecognizably ugly and depraved, while the oil portrait has recovered its pristine beauty. It is a brilliant fable.

On publication in magazine form in America in July

1890, the reception of the story was surprisingly positive. Recognizing the old morality tales of the selling of the soul, and the wages of sin, reviewers were a little uneasy (was it necessary to make Dorian's unspecified sins *quite* so compelling?) but generally persuaded by the tale's apparent rectitude. Wilde was mildly chagrined by the approbation: any author who could so easily please the American public ought to mend his ways. 'Yes,' he agreed, 'there is a terrible moral in *Dorian Gray* – a moral which the prurient will not be able to find in it, but which will be revealed to all those whose minds are healthy. Is this an artistic error? I fear it is. It is the only error in the book.'

Not that *Dorian Gray* was a book, but it was soon to become one. The small English publisher Ward, Lock & Co. asked Wilde if they might publish it the following year. The only problem, they believed, was that at 50,000 words the story was too short to justify itself as a single volume. Wilde agreed to write six additional chapters, and welcomed the opportunity to revise the text. The additional chapters benefited the novel considerably, adding weight to the characterization, and making the plot both more interesting and more plausible.

Buoyed by the favourable American reviews of the Lippincott's version of the story, its author felt confident about the reception of the forthcoming book. But a number of hostile notices had already appeared, and his publisher was concerned about the reception of the novel in England.

Wilde was defiant, if slightly disingenuous: 'Each man sees his own sins in Dorian Gray. What Dorian Gray's sins are no one knows. He who finds them has brought them.' Strongly prompted by Ward, Lock, though, Wilde amended a number of passages from the 1890 text, particularly those which suggested homoerotic themes. He hated the process: 'It has bothered me terribly,' he said, reminding the publishers that it was his book, and not theirs. But he reluctantly agreed to a number of crucial amendments. The male characters become less physically demonstrative with each other, and the possible implications of certain key passages are removed. In the 1890 text, when Basil Hallward inquires of Dorian, 'Why is your friendship so fateful to young men?' Dorian declines to justify himself, allowing the implication of sexual misconduct. In the later version, however, Dorian rebuts the charge.

The Picture of Dorian Gray was published in April of 1891, a handsome volume like all of Wilde's works, for he insisted on some control of the processes of design, typography and binding. Designed by his friend Charles Ricketts, the book had grey-brown paper-covered boards, with a gilt-stamped vellum spine, and was issued in a regular edition of 1,000 copies at six shillings and a large paper edition of 250 copies, signed by Oscar, at two guineas. Like its hero, *Dorian* looks terrific if it can unnaturally preserve its youth, but deteriorates badly with use. The gilt fades, the boards get soiled and dirty, the joints and edges crack and reveal their tawdry underpinnings. In the rare book market, fine copies are virtually unknown, and if one were found in the exceptionally uncommon dust jacket, it would be worth some £30,000 ($54,000).

However pretty the book, and however attractive its apparent moral, English reviewers were by no means as receptive as their American counterparts. Perhaps this was because the topic of male sexual love was a potently forbidden one in English society. Men educated at public schools – English literary culture consisted almost entirely of them – had been incessantly warned by their schoolmasters, in coded but instantly recognizable language, of the appalling effects of the vices of masturbation and homosexuality. Presumably Americans were too busy killing bears and building railroads to worry much about such piffling dangers. English reviewers, though, frequently regarded it as their business to be on the watch for signs of scandalous behaviour, if only because they knew there was so much of it about. Homosexuality was rife in literary culture, but discreet: the problem with *Dorian Gray* was not that it was explicit, but that its allusions were so obvious that any man of good education and wide reading could not miss what was going on.

The *Daily Chronicle* labelled the novel 'a tale spawned from the leprous literature of the French Decadents . . . a poisonous book, the atmosphere of which is heavy with the mephitic odours of moral and spiritual putrefaction'. Well, one might reply, that's the point, isn't it? But it wasn't. The point was that it was wicked to allow the attractions of such vices, even in order to condemn them. Presumably it gave comfort to the enemy.

And it did, it did. *Dorian Gray* may have caused pain and outrage elsewhere, but it went down a treat in Oxford, that traditional home for refined homosexuals. The high priest of the aesthetic movement, Wilde's Oxford mentor Walter Pater, had declined to review the Lippincott's *Dorian*, regarding it as dangerous, but was deeply enthusiastic about the book version, calling it 'a vivid, though carefully considered, exposure of the corruption of a soul'. The poet Lionel Johnson gave a copy to Lord Alfred Douglas, an undergraduate at Magdalen (which was Wilde's college) and the youngest son of the Marquess of Queensberry.

It would not be an understatement to say that Bosie, as he was known, fell in love with the novel. He read it, according to his own testimony, nine times straight through, though other reports claim it was fourteen, but not in a row. Contemporary photographs show a languid youth, slight, graceful and blond, with a face in which petulance and conceit combine, and whose bodily demeanour suggests both sensuousness and a coiled tension. None of the surviving photos suggests a happy young man, but this was not, perhaps, the image he was trying to project. He was wanton, thoroughly spoiled, regarded as something of a beauty by his (male) friends, and used to getting what he wanted. He wanted to meet Oscar Wilde.

Flattered by Bosie's rank and intrigued by tales of his beauty, Wilde soon entertained Lord Alfred Douglas in his Tite Street house, and inscribed for his acolyte a copy, dated 1 July 1891, of the signed limited edition of *Dorian Gray*. (I'm not sure what this would be worth, but it is one of the most perfect books imaginable. I would confidently pay £60,000 ($110,000) for it, and be certain of some profit.)

Though Wilde's marriage to Constance was deemed a happy one, and devoted as he was to his two young sons, he was by this time an active homosexual, having been seduced by Robert Ross at Oxford some five years earlier. For the previous few years he had been having a relationship with John Gray, whose name Dorian takes. But with the coming of Bosie, a real Dorian was about to enter his life, someone whose idea of himself had been confirmed and accentuated by Wilde's novel. *The Picture of Dorian Gray* became a script for Bosie, paralleling the way in which Dorian's life is irretrievably altered by the dangerous French book given him by the cynical Lord Henry Wotton.

Oscar was to become both Bosie's mentor and his lover, and Bosie was to lead Oscar, willingly, to destruction. It was a perfect case of life imitating art. As the artist Basil Hallward reflects, having met Dorian and painted his portrait:

> I have always been my own master; had at least always been so till I met Dorian Gray . . . Something seemed to tell me I was on the verge of a terrible crisis in my life. I had a strange feeling that Fate had in store for me exquisite joys and exquisite sorrows.

One would be delighted at the perfection of the symmetry were it not so sad a story.

We know what happens from here: under the influence of Douglas, Wilde's flowering and ascendancy; the enraged visit of the Marquess of Queensberry with his calling card addressed to Wilde 'posing as a somdomite'; Wilde's counter-suit, at Douglas's insistence; the three trials, and Wilde's incarceration; the unhappy final years of exile until the sadness of his death in a Paris hotel room in November of 1900. The story is so well known as to suggest a kind of inevitability; but virtually from the beginning Wilde's foolish devotion to Bosie was recognized by those around him – even by himself – as likely to have catastrophic results.

At the trials in 1895, *The Picture of Dorian Gray* was produced by the prosecution as evidence of Wilde's immorality. Sir Edward Carson, who had been at school with Wilde in Ireland, maintained that '*Dorian Gray* is a book which it can be conclusively proved advocates the vice imputed to Mr Wilde.' It is a crude line of thought – though ironically a true one – and Oscar, from the witness box, made mincemeat of his adversary. He was playing on his home ground, for the question of the relations between life and art were ones on which he had thought deeply and eloquently. He frequently made Carson look a fool with his perfectly formed rebuttals. In answer to Carson's charge that the novel was perverse and likely to pervert, Wilde answered haughtily that such a conclusion 'could only be to brutes and illiterates. The views of Philistines on art are incalculably stupid.'

Not as stupid, you may think, as saying this in a courtroom in which a group of such Philistines was sitting in judgement upon him. But Oscar could never resist an epigram; it was the temptation he most loved giving in to. As he acknowledged in a letter to Conan Doyle:

I throw probability out of the window for the sake of a phrase, and the chance of an epigram makes me desert truth. The newspapers seem to be written by the prurient for the Philistine. I cannot understand how they can treat *Dorian Gray* as immoral.

Yet Oscar deserted truth pretty comprehensively at his trials, and was conclusively exposed as a practitioner of unnatural vices with assorted rent boys. But none of those partners, whom Oscar treated kindly, served him more ignominiously than the ghastly Bosie. Even after the diminished and humiliated Oscar slunk off to France for his final years, he was dogged by Bosie, and foolishly resumed relations with him, causing the long-suffering Constance finally to withdraw his allowance. To the end, poor foolish Oscar pursued his beautiful young man, even once he had recognized the contamination of spirit that lay within. History has been too kind to him: he, of all people, should have known better. It is hard to escape the conclusion, that, delightful as he was, Oscar Wilde was a damn fool. It's hard to know what to make of folly on this scale; there's something grandly operatic about it. How could Oscar's sad fate have been averted, given that he seems to have chosen it so wantonly? We may conclude, I suppose, that character is destiny, or (at the very least) that vulnerable romantics should avoid dinners with American publishers. You can never tell what they may lead to.

ON THE ROAD

There is an old riddle that goes: 'What is black and white and re(a)d all over?' The answer to which – in those times before colour print in journalism – is, of course, a newspaper. The question, which has long ceased to amuse even children, reminds me, though, of a recent object that caused quite a stir at auction: a 120-foot long roll of teletype paper, nine inches wide, imprinted with greyish black markings, which looks, from a certain distance, like an installation forged by the combined imaginations of Cy Twombly and Richard Long. Its creator (called 'an action painter' by Norman Mailer) described his method as 'sketching' and regarded the object as 'like a road,' which, from that certain distance, it palpably was. And that, of course, could hardly have been more appropriate, because the scroll was actually an elongated literary manuscript, written by Jack Kerouac in six caffeine-laced weeks in 1951, and published six years later as *On the Road*.

In fact, though, *On the Road* was a long time in the making. Its subject, he said in a letter to its hero, Neal Cassady (Sal Paradise in the novel) was:

girls, weed, etc. Story deals with you and me and the road . . . how we first met 1947, early days; Denver 47 etc.; 1949 trip in Hudson; that summer in queer Plymouth and 110 mi-an-hour Caddy and Chi and Detroit; and final trip to Mexico . . . Plot, if any, is devoted to your development from young jailkid of early days to later (present) W.C. Fields saintliness . . . I've telled all the road now. Went fast because road is fast.

Kerouac began work on the novel in 1948, rewrote it entirely, then produced the long draft on that single roll of paper, then tinkered with the result during the six long years it took to get the book published (during which time he wrote twelve further books). In spite of the success of his relatively conventional first novel, *The Town and the City*, in 1951, publishers were wary of the unrestrained hyperactivity of the new work. It was hard to recall anything quite like this boyish voyage of discovery:

Man, wow, there's so many things to do, so many things to write
How to even *begin* to get it all down and without

modified restraints and all hung-up on like literary inhibitions and grammatical fears . . . I took a big swig in the wild, lyrical, drizzling air of Nebraska.

'Whooeee, here we go!'

I said to myself 'Wow, what'll *Denver* be like!'

The use of the exclamation marks suggests the child-like exuberance of a comic book – 'Golly gosh, Batman!' – rather than the prose of a serious novel. *'Denver!'* You had to be seriously overfuelled with adrenaline to get a kick out of Denver in 1947.

The book's topics were suggested by the spontaneous outspokenness of its prose: getting stoned, getting drunk, getting laid, getting *somewhere*. And yet there was, strictly, no destination on this journey. Kerouac famously had nowhere to go, no home save that with his adored mama (MéMere), to whom he remained for a lifetime Ti Jean.

I have in stock, at the moment, a long letter from Kerouac to his mother, which makes it clear that, if he was ever going to settle down, it would only be with her. Writing from San Luis Obispo in April of 1953, he extols the beauties of California, and suggests his mother join him there. San Luis Obispo, he enthuses, has two (!) television stations, and a great climate!

The best idea I think will be for us to start in a trailer, for about a year, till we get a start . . .

Remember, quit when you've had enuf, all we have to do is make a start here in a trailer, an old trailer. The rest can come later – you'll see I'm right – you'll see I'm right.

This depressing little letter gives no indication of the extraordinary life he was leading at the time, nor of the wide-ranging erotic opportunities available to him. Presumably even living with his mama in a trailer wouldn't have cramped his style. He was a visitor to any number of women, and more regularly to Burroughs, Carl Solomon, Cassady, Ginsberg: the literary brat pack that assembled round him. He came to visit, stayed until he was sick of them, or they of him, and moved on, making ends meet by casual labour, writing, writing all the time.

It was the journey that mattered, delineating and transgressing frontiers, relentlessly seeking out the new. The goal was an inward one, enhanced by carousing and reflecting, in search of that fabled moment of total awareness and harmony. *On the Road* was originally entitled *The Beat Generation,* which seemed, properly, to suggest an amalgam of rhythm, aggression and fatigue. But Kerouac later insisted that it was simply a short-hand term for those seeking the beatific. Soon enough a *San Francisco Chronicle* journalist coined the term 'beatnik' (like Sputnik, get it?) which Kerouac loathed, and which caught on a treat.

The manuscript was turned down all over town. It had its supporters, like the prescient Robert Giroux, but most publishing houses were not interested. Publishers, of course, are a notoriously unadventurous lot, but Kerouac's friends didn't like the early drafts of the book either. Even Ginsberg didn't. Though he was enthusiastic about the nature of the project, his reservations were so profound as to seem to undermine the sincerity of his praise.

> I am worried about the whole book. It's crazy (not merely inspired crazy) but unrelated crazy . . . crazy in a bad way, and *got*, aesthetically and publishing-wise, to be pulled back together, re constructed. I can't see anyone, New Directions, Europe, putting it out as it is. They wont, they wont.

Kerouac was devastated, and felt betrayed to the very core. His response didn't pull any punches:

> I see it now, why it is great and why you hate it . . . You . . . are a disbeliever, a hater, your giggles don't fool me, I see the snarl under it . . . Go blow your Corsos . . . I hope he sinks a knife in you . . . Leave me alone . . . and don't ever darken me again.

It was Malcolm Cowley, one of the great diviners and encouragers of literary talent, who eventually recognized the qualities of the book, and recommended it to Viking. But first, Cowley thought, sections of the text needed to be published in magazines, to get the reading public used to Kerouac. And the text, he added firmly, needed serious revision:

> It had swung back and forth between the East Coast and West Coast like a huge pendulum. I thought that some of the trips should be telescoped, and Kerouac agreed and did the job . . . All the changes I suggested were big ones, mostly omissions. I said why don't you boil down these to two or three trips and keep the mood of the content.

When the book was finally published, on 5 September 1957, it became the talk of New York – and in literary terms the talk of New York is the talk of America – through one great piece of good luck. *The New York Times*, both the recorder and the arbiter of much that is thought and felt in New York, published a rave review by Gilbert Millstein. *On the Road,* he maintained, was an 'authentic work of art', the publication of which represented an 'historic occasion':

> the fact is that 'On the Road' is the most beautifully executed, the clearest and the most important utterance yet made by the generation Kerouac himself

54

named years ago as 'beat,' and whose principal avatar he is. Just as, more than any other novel of the Twenties, 'The Sun Also Rises' came to be regarded as the testament of the 'Lost Generation,' so it seems certain that 'On the Road' will come to be known as that of the 'Beat Generation.'

Everybody rushed out to buy the book, hardly pausing to ask the obvious question: who the hell was Gilbert Millstein? *The Times* regular book reviewer, the conservative and crusty Orville Prescott, would not normally have chosen to review such a book. But he was on holiday. When he returned to the paper, Prescott was livid, and Millstein never reviewed another book in the daily *Times*.

Millstein's review guaranteed that *On the Road* would be noticed – which is the major desideratum in New York – but not that it would be admired. A fierce debate ensued. In a much-quoted mot, Truman Capote called it 'typing, not writing'; John Updike parodied it in *The New Yorker*; and Norman Mailer (in *Advertisements for Myself*) called Kerouac 'sentimental as a lollipop' and 'pretentious as a rich whore'. He was rather sorry afterwards, and put his spleen down to the reaction of a writer made uneasy by the advent of something genuinely new: 'I read it with a sinking heart. We were very competitive back then. I was thinking, Oh shit, this guy's done it. He was there, living it, and I was just an intellectual, writing about it.'

None of that mattered: when you get Truman Capote, John Updike and Norman Mailer arguing about you, you've already got it made. The book was reprinted only two weeks after publication, and a third printing followed almost immediately. For a brief period of five weeks, the book even hit the *Times* best-seller list. Kerouac had much to thank the obscure Gordon Millstein for, as Millstein himself recalled: 'he made no bones about it, either. He'd put his arm around me and say "This is Gilbert Millstein – he made me."'

Because of that fortuitous single review in *The New York Times,* America had heard of the Beat Generation, and Kerouac was regarded as its spokesman. He hated it: 'I am being destroyed,' he wrote, 'by well meaning admirers . . . they have no conception of how much they outnumber me and all their enthusiasm and mail piles up meanwhile with further demands from every-where including insane 10,000 word letters from girls who try to write in subterranean style.'

It was clear that the good-looking, brilliantly louche Kerouac was someone from whom you had to protect your daughters, and he was duly, and publicly, reviled. *Time Magazine,* that traditional voice of middle-America, declared the book hedonistic and degenerate, decried its disregard for social custom and morality, was repelled by its 'dionysian revels'. *On the Road*, it concluded, was both dangerous and subversive. And so intelligent young people all over America devoured it greedily, discovering in it not merely a new set of temptations, but also something positive and pure. As Kerouac was later to describe it: 'a picture about good-hearted kids in pain of soul doing wild things out of desperation'.

The literature of the 1950s was much more radical than that generated by the apparently more subversive decade, the sixties. *Catcher in the Rye* (1951), *Howl* (1955), *The Naked Lunch* (1955), *On the Road* (1957) charted areas of disaffection which were profoundly shocking to that peaceable postwar American generation that wanted little more than a new tract house, a safe job and a snappy car, a presentably compliant spouse and kids.

The male writers of the fifties were living a form of life which could hardly be copied, and for which a buttoned-up ('silent') generation of youngsters was not ready. In contrast, the literature of the sixties – one thinks of Kesey, Vonnegut, Tom Wolfe – invited the young to come out and join the fun. It was about *you* – who you could become, if you only turned on, and simultaneously dropped out and dropped in.

The world of the beats, though, was less comfortable, more foreign and more dangerous, peopled by mental patients, drug addicts, queers, criminals: a lot

57

of them smart as hell, and who didn't give a damn what other people thought. These were no hippies, mere consumers of a new style and culture. You couldn't just grow your hair, change your wardrobe, pick up a few easy new ideas and habits. There were no styles and no rules, no role models.

When Allen Ginsberg claimed to have seen the best minds of his generation destroyed, he was not referring to those resolutely undestroyed professors who had guided him at Columbia, to Lionel Trilling or Jacques Barzun. Instead he had in mind, say, Carl Solomon, whom he had met in mental hospital, and who was under the clear impression that he was a character in a Russian novel, the heroin addict William Burroughs, and Neal Cassady, the crazed poet manqué of San Francisco. It was Jack Kerouac who stood at the pivotal centre of the ill-formed group, and it is in *On the Road* that so many of them are enshrined. Today the novel sells about 125,000 copies a year, and total sales are approaching four million copies.

So when that 120-foot roll of manuscript came up for auction on 22 May 2001, Christie's made sure that there was plenty of fuss. After all, manuscripts of twentieth-century literature have a poor history at auction. I can't think of a single manuscript by a living author that has made as much as £100,000 ($180,000) in the rooms, and the record price for a twentieth-century manuscript was for Kafka's *The Trial*, at one million pounds. (Still cheap, it seems to me: for that money you can't buy even a bad Jasper Johns.) So the Christie's publicity machine went into overdrive: the major newspapers and magazines helped rope in prospective purchasers, and the sale was covered by TV and radio. The eventual buyer, at $2,430,000 was one James Irsay, unknown to the world of book collecting, but a figure of some celebrity as the owner of the Indianapolis Colts football team. (By a nice apparent coincidence, Kerouac was a talented football player, who played for Columbia until he decided to quit. By way of explanation, the coach said 'Kerouac is tired.') Irsay, who has plans to take the manuscript in a car trip round America in a re-enactment of *On the Road*, was modest about his acquisition, which he thought quite reasonably priced. 'I look on it as a stewardship. I don't believe you own anything. In this world, it's dust to dust.'

In the meantime, one hopes he is looking after the fragile manuscript under carefully modulated archival conditions, lest his words become true sooner than he envisages.

ULYSSES

Dennis Silverman, gambler, gourmand, and bon viveur, was an imposing figure of something over thirty stone, an amiable fellow with the accent and demeanour of a Damon Runyon huckster. He was in control of one of the local branches of the New York City Teamsters' Union Pension Fund, which may just have accounted for the giant rolls of hundred dollar bills he carried in his capacious front pockets, and which he was good at spending. He was eventually indicted for fraud, was too ill to stand trial, and died in Florida in 1995. He owned the finest James Joyce collection of his generation.

Uneasy at rare book fairs, where he mistakenly thought himself surrounded by people of learning and gentility, he tended to spend a few tens of thousands of dollars quickly but cannily, and then look for an agreeable partner for dinner. One year – sometime in the late eighties – it happened to be me. Over a lavish Chinese meal, seated at a table for eight (large enough to hold the flock of ducks he wished to consume), he told me proudly about the scope of his collection.

'I got great stuff. I got da *Pawtrait of da Ahtist*, inscribed by Joyce to Harriet Weaver, da *Dubliners* inscribed to his mothah-in-law, and da *Ulysses* to Mawgrat Andason . . .'

Now these are mighty books, and I was not foolish enough to suppose Dennis incapable of appreciating them. He was a smart guy, was playing the book market shrewdly, and bought only the best. Whether he knew much about their contents was a different question.

'But Dennis,' I asked, 'have you read them?'

He looked shocked. 'I read da *Dubliners*!' he said firmly.

'What did you think of it?'

He was disappointed to hear me ask such a dumb question.

'A mastapiece!' he said. 'Den I read da *Pawtrait*!'

'And?'

'Whaddya mean? It's wondaful!'

Clearly this guy wasn't just fooling around.

'What do you think of *Ulysses*?' I asked.

'I'm on Chaptah Faw,' he said, looking a little uneasy.

'And?'

'I don' like da details!'

Though I have read the book many times, and

revere it accordingly, I could sympathize. As Dr Johnson said in another context, no one has ever wished it longer than it is. The sacred realm of academics and exegetes since its publication in 1922, *Ulysses* is universally admired, but rarely loved. That it is the acknowledged masterpiece of twentieth-century literature only serves to remind us of what an unsatisfactory category 'masterpiece' can be.

'Ah, Dennis,' I said sympathetically, 'it's all details.'

'I know,' he said sadly. 'You want some mor'a dese ducks?'

Dennis bought his copy of *Ulysses* at the sale of the books of the late James Gilvarry, in 1986, for \$35,000 (£19,400). At the time, it seemed a lot of money, but it was not only one of the 100 copies signed by Joyce, it also bore a presentation inscription by him. I know of only one other copy in private hands that is both signed and inscribed.

Like all of Joyce's work, *Ulysses* was a long time gestating. The initial idea was conceived in 1906, when Joyce told his brother Stanislaus that he was contemplating a short story about a Jewish Dubliner with an unfaithful wife, who clearly prefigures Leopold Bloom, the protagonist of *Ulysses*. The story was intended for inclusion in *Dubliners* (which was published in 1914), though Joyce hadn't yet written it.

In that same year, Joyce began the first substantial work on *Ulysses*. The idea was at once simple, and infinitely complex: it tells the comprehensive story of a day in the life of Leopold Bloom, a commercial traveller, whose peregrinations and trials throughout Dublin on 16 June 1904 are intended to parallel those of that other heroic exile, Ulysses himself. The method (later described, somewhat misleadingly, as 'stream of consciousness') gives us an uncensored and apparently unmediated entry into the moment-by-moment apprehensions of its hero – and into the minds, too, of Stephen Daedalus, whom we first met in *A Portrait of the Artist as a Young Man*, in 1916, and of Bloom's wife, Molly.

Joyce was clear that the book, from its inception, was encyclopaedically ambitious, and would take years to complete: 'It is impossible for me to write these episodes quickly. The elements needed will fuse only after a prolonged existence together. I confess that it is an extremely tiresome book but it is the only book which I am able to write at present.' But while those episodes were quietly fusing away, it was necessary to eat, as well as to write, and despite the generosity of Joyce's patrons he was constantly hard up. He regarded it as his right to live well, and the more money he was given, the more he spent.

The answer lay with Ezra Pound, whose enthusiasm, editorial and entrepreneurial energy were as generously on offer to Joyce, as they were to Eliot and to Hemingway. Pound suggested sending the chapters of the book – called 'episodes', and titled after their Homeric equivalents – to small, modernist magazines for publication. Frequently run by proprietors of independent means, some of them paid surprisingly generously.

Both of Joyce's previous books had suffered at the hands of the censors and nay-sayers, and if his masterpiece was going to see the light of day, it would only be through private sources, both of funding and of publication. For both he was to rely on women publishers who believed in him passionately, and were prepared to face the consequences of issuing such a controversial and explicit work. Intelligent women were then much less squeamish about sexual matters than was (or is) supposed. Without the support of Margaret Anderson, Harriet Weaver and Sylvia Beach there might well have been no *Ulysses*; at the very least, its publication would have been delayed by many years.

In March of 1918, Pound sent an episode to Margaret Anderson and Jane Heap at *The Little Review*. Anderson was immediately entranced: 'This is the most beautiful thing we'll ever have. We'll print it if it's the last effort of our lives.' Over the next few years, regular pieces from *Ulysses* appeared in the magazine. But in January 1920, the issue containing 'Cyclops' was confiscated for obscenity by US Customs. Over the next months, Miss Anderson published further bits of *Ulysses*, notwithstanding the harassment of the censors.

At the subsequent trial of the magazine, in February of 1921, the judge urged that Miss Anderson should not be present in the courtroom when the allegedly obscene passages were read aloud. 'I am sure,' he said gallantly, 'she didn't know the significance of what she was publishing.' However insufferable the tone, he was partly right. She had, of course, read what she had published, but how could *she* tell, she asked her lawyer, the book collector John Quinn, if it was *legally* obscene? He, with lawyerly caution, admitted he didn't know either, but that she should stop doing it in future. (He later bought the manuscript of the book from Joyce for $5,000 (£2,700).)

At much the same time, a similarly undaunted woman publisher, Harriet Weaver, agreed to pay £50 ($90) for the right to publish episodes in her London magazine, *The Egoist*, with an eye to publishing the book in its entirety some time later. She had previously published *A Portrait of the Artist as a Young Man*, in 1917, and had the not very convincing idea of eventually publishing Joyce's new work under the title *A Portrait of the Artist*. Though *The Egoist* published five episodes, Miss Weaver could not find a printer willing to take on the book. Printers and publishers alike were afraid of it: both Huebsch and Boni and Liveright in America, and the Hogarth Press in England, all rejected it. (Virginia Woolf estimated that it would have taken a professional typesetter two years just to set it.)

Because it was widely circulated as work-in-progress, *Ulysses* gripped an international audience of sophisticated readers well before it was published as a book, a nice case of the tentacles appearing before the octopus. Joyce's contemporaries responded as if the forthcoming novel were a touchstone designed to test and reveal their natures, as their comments revealed:

Gertrude Stein: 'But who came first, Gertrude Stein or James Joyce?'
Ernest Hemingway: 'Joyce has a most goddamn wonderful book.'
T.S. Eliot: 'I wish, for my own sake, that I had not read it.'
Virginia Woolf: 'The book of a self-taught working man . . . a queasy undergraduate scratching his pimples.'
Ezra Pound: 'Well, Mr Joyce, I recon you're a damn fine writer, that's what I recon . . . You can take it from me, an' I'm a jedge.'

Joyce had shone a torch into a previously shuttered internal world; in doing so, he revealed his readers to themselves. In modern literary culture, *Ulysses* was the most discussed work of the period. But still there was no book.

At this critical moment appeared Miss Sylvia Beach, a young American of modest means but great ambitions, who had opened the bookshop Shakespeare and Company on the left bank in Paris. Miss Beach had never published a book before, and had little idea of how to go about it. But, she asked Joyce earnestly, 'Would you let Shakespeare and Co. have the honour of bringing out your *Ulysses*?' Joyce was delighted, and quickly settled a deal whereby he received 66 per cent of the profits. Miss Beach's business partner, Adrienne Monnier, introduced her to the Dijon printer Darantiere, who seemed a perfect man for the job, partly (if inconveniently) because he spoke no English.

His patience, and Miss Beach's purse, were stretched to the limit by Joyce's method of composition, which worked on a practice of slow and inexorable accretion, like a glacier. Hating to think of the text as finished, he never stopped revising. *Ulysses* increased in size by a third as Joyce added to, amended, and corrected the proofs. Darantiere reset the type, not always transcribing Joyce's minute hand accurately. Miss Beach worried, and paid. On 2 February 1922 – Joyce's birthday – the first two copies of *Ulysses* arrived at the Gare du Nord from Dijon, where the train was met by Miss Beach, who delivered the copies to the

Joyces' flat. It was a momentous day in the history of literature. It is said that Joyce immediately inscribed a copy to Nora, who soon sold it to John Quinn, but since this copy has never been located, the story may be apocryphal.

It was a good few weeks before further copies were provided and Miss Beach could put them out for sale. Some had been pre-sold by subscription, others went quickly, even at prices that were high for the time. The 750 regular copies, in their Aegean blue wrappers, sold for 150 francs. A further 150 copies, printed on Verge d'Arches in deference to the French taste for *grands papiers*, were priced at 250 francs. And best of all were the 100 copies, signed by Joyce, at 350 francs. Dennis Silverman's copy (Number 3) was soon to be inscribed by Joyce to the brave Margaret Anderson.

Ulysses was no sooner published than banned in both England and America. But it kept selling. A second edition of 2,000 copies, printed by the Egoist Press, was issued later in 1922 at two guineas, much to the disgust of Miss Beach. Apparently Miss Weaver had put up the money for the printing of the Shakespeare edition, and felt entitled to issue her own edition, using the same plates, and bound identically (though in a slightly different size). Joyce had concurred in the decision to issue this cheaper edition, but Sylvia felt betrayed. She had published the book more expensively, and booksellers who had bought her copy (and still had it on their shelves) were dismayed to find a cheaper version offered so quickly. Relations between Joyce and Miss Beach never entirely recovered.

The third edition of 500 copies, also printed by the Egoist in 1923, was impounded and destroyed by English Customs at Folkestone. Though 499 copies were said to have been destroyed, we have had three copies through our hands – one of them in the original binding, two rebound – and have located three others.

Over the next decade, *Ulysses* had to be smuggled into England and America, until it was eventually seized by US Customs. It was tried for obscenity in 1933, before Justice John M. Woolsey, a judge of the US District Court. In a judgement remarkable for its understanding of the aims and methods of the book, the judge concluded that, however sexually explicit the novel was, he could not detect anywhere in it 'the leer of the sensualist'. His decision that *Ulysses* was safe for American consumption was long-sighted and right-minded, though curiously argued: 'whilst in many places the effect of *Ulysses* on the reader is somewhat emetic, nowhere does it tend to be an aphrodisiac. *Ulysses* may, therefore, be admitted into the United States.' Which is to say, from a legal point of view, it may make you vomit, but it won't give you an erection, so that's all right then. (Which continues to be the American attitude to censorship of television and film.)

I don't know if Dennis Silverman ever finished reading *Ulysses* and, if he did, whether it made him feel sick or sexy. It certainly increased his riches: when he came to sell the book in 1991 he made a cool $100,000 (£55,500) profit. I'm rather pleased, for Dennis's sake, that he wasn't at the sale of the library of Roger Rechler at Christie's in 2002, when the second and lesser inscribed 1/100 (given by Joyce to the obscure Henry Kaeser) made some $460,000 (£255,500). It was, by far, the greatest price achieved for a twentieth-century book. It should be. It is the greatest twentieth-century book.

Joyce, who saw, and knew, and anticipated everything, worried that *Ulysses* was in danger from the moment of publication of being eclipsed by the admiration of its readers. That it would be valued, rather than read – a process that reaches its apotheosis with the Silverman copy. When Joyce's rapt acolyte, Stuart Gilbert, presented him with cuttings of the first reviews, which were uniformly, if not always positively, awestruck, Joyce seemed a little disappointed. 'Doesn't anyone think it's funny?' he asked, plaintively. The answer was no, hardly anybody. Despite what Joyce thought of as its sane and joyful spirit, it isn't that sort of masterpiece, and one would feel a little uneasy putting it beside, say, *Tristram Shandy*, *Don Quixote* or *Huckleberry Finn*. It made Joyce's reputation, to be sure, as well as that of a library full of later scholars, editors, and close readers. But Dennis Silverman was right, in his homely way. *Ulysses* wears you out. I own, and treasure, an inscribed copy of the 1/750 first edition of *Ulysses*, which will stay in fine condition as long as I don't read it. It is one of the pleasures of advancing age that I'm not even tempted.

SONS AND LOVERS

The novelist Dennis Wheatley, thriller writer, Satanist, erotomane, and bore, was (somewhat surprisingly) a collector of first editions. Blackwell's catalogue of his library, issued in 1979, ran to 2,274 items, and included much of the author's research material, many of the books bearing Wheatley's pompous pencilled note 'used by me in writing *The Devil Burps Twice*', or some such bit of prime psychic inflation.

A few of the choicest items, however, were sold before the catalogue was issued. I was lucky enough to buy the best of these: a copy of the first edition of D.H. Lawrence's *Sons and Lovers*, in the dustwrapper. The wrapper was unprepossessing, and missing a small portion of the front panel. It cost £400 ($700), which was rather a lot, but I was an avid book collector in those days, and it immediately became the jewel of my not very distinguished Lawrence collection. Though I was told, at the time, that there were a couple of other examples of the dustwrapper, I never managed to locate where they were. And it is one of the striking oddities of the trade in modern books that the dust-wrapper of a book is worth ten times – sometimes much more – than the book itself. Books without their wrappers are regarded as incomplete, which seems a little silly, as if they were Chippendale chairs, without legs. Nor was this wrapper particularly attractive, though it did include a 'brief notice' which is now reckoned to be by Lawrence himself. The front panel reads:

> Mr D.H. Lawrence's new novel covers a wide field: life in a colliery, on a farm, in a manufacturing centre. It is concerned with the contrasted outlook on life of two generations. The title, *Sons and Lovers*, indicates the conflicting claims of a young man's mother and sweetheart for predominance.

The blurb is cunningly rich in implication, for *Sons and Lovers* has a doubly distinctive place in English literature. It is one of the earliest novels to use psycho-analysis as an organizing principle, and it is the first great novel about working-class life, written by, as it were, an insider.

Born in 1885, the son of a Nottinghamshire coal miner who married a woman of petit bourgeois background and aspiration, the precocious young Lawrence steeped himself in literature, reading widely and voraciously. It would be a mistake to regard him as some sort of freakish autodidact. In fact, Eastwood had an active literary culture, and Lawrence received a high quality education, which culminated in matriculation at Nottingham University College in 1906, after coming first in the entrance exam.

After leaving Nottingham with a first class degree, he spent a few unhappy years teaching in Croydon. He published *The White Peacock* in 1911, and *The Trespasser* in 1912, to favourable receptions, but they did not generate enough income to live on. He'd had an advance of £50 ($90) on the first novel, which prompted an incredulous response from his father: 'and tha's niver done a day's work in tha' life!' Returning for a brief visit to Eastwood in March of 1912, he visited his favourite university professor, Ernest Weekley, who had a young and thoroughly attractive wife, Frieda von Richthofen. Six weeks later Lawrence and Frieda (leaving behind her young children) had eloped for the continent. He brought with him the unfinished manuscript of *Sons and Lovers*.

He'd been unable to finish the book. It had been intended as the story of his coming of age, but neither the growing up nor the novel had gone smoothly. Lawrence had found himself, in adolescence, torn between the fierce ambition of his mother and the competing claims of his first love, Jessie Chambers, who had helped him with the early versions of the text. He had come to believe that he would never be free to love while his mother was alive. His life had been appropriated by her.

As if in unconscious acknowledgement, Lydia Lawrence died, in 1911. It allowed Lawrence to begin to write his own story, but he was so paralysed by the horror of her death, and the deadening presence of her absence, that he couldn't make much progress. After Frieda stormed into his life he was able to complete the book, though his mother continued to be its dominating presence. Poor Jessie Chambers was horrified when she read it, believing that Lawrence had betrayed their relationship, and himself, in accepting his mother's point of view. Many years later, Lawrence was to agree: he had thought his mother was right, but, he came to realize, he had merely colluded with her in the banishment of his father.

Paul Morel (as the novel was originally entitled) was, he recognized, the best thing he had done: 'I tell you it has got form – form: haven't I made it patiently, out of sweat as well as blood . . . Read my novel. It's a great novel. If you can't see the development – which is slow, like growth – I can.'

This letter was written in November of 1912 to Edward Garnett, to whom Lawrence had been introduced by Ford Madox Ford in 1911. Garnett, himself a novelist, acted as reader for a number of publishers, and was a better editor than he was a writer. Though he was talking a good game, Lawrence was, in fact, worried about the fate of his manuscript, which had just been rejected by Heinemann, the publisher of his first two novels. Mr Heinemann ('may his name be used as a curse') thought the novel improper.

> I feel that the book is unsatisfactory . . . its want of reticence makes it unfit, I fear, for publication in England as things are. The tyranny of the libraries is such that a book far less outspoken would certainly be damned . . .

Lawrence, as he soon confessed to Garnett, was that little bit disappointed by the response; given that he had a distinctly inflated sense of his mission:

> Why, why was I born an Englishman! – my cursed, rotten-boned, pappy-hearted countrymen, *why* was I sent to *them*. Christ on the cross must have hated his countrymen . . . Curse the blasted, jelly-boned swines, the slimy belly-wriggling invertebrates, the miserable sodding rotters, the flaming sods, the snivelling, dribbling, dithering palsied pulse-less lot that make up England . . . God, how I hate them! God curse them – funkers. God blast them, wish-wash. Exterminate them, slime.

Makes Conrad's Mr Kurtz seem a liberal spirit, doesn't it? This torrent of invective satisfyingly purged,

Lawrence was immediately pacified by Garnett, who helped him edit the book into publishable form.

Lawrence was by this time happily resident in Gargano, Italy, swooningly in the arms of Frieda, and already beginning the sequence of love poems that was to be published in 1916 as *Look! We Have Come Through!* (Which caused the fastidious Bertrand Russell to remark that they may have come through, but he didn't see why he had to look.)

Even Frieda sometimes found the tumultuous Lawrence tough going. She had helped him to finish the final draft of *Sons and Lovers:*

> I lived and suffered that book, and wrote bits of it when he would ask me 'What do you think my mother felt like then?' I had to go deeply into the character of Miriam and all the others; and when he wrote his mother's death he was ill with grief and his grief made me ill too . . . Towards the end of *Sons and Lovers* I got fed up and turned against all this 'house of Atreus' feeling, and I wrote a skit called *Paul Morel, or his Mother's Darling.* He read it and said, coldly: 'This kind of thing isn't called a skit.'

However little he liked being teased, Lawrence had found in Frieda – as again in Garnett – a perfect person to provide the support, encouragement, and loving engagement to finish his novel. Garnett cut about ten per cent of the final manuscript version, much to its benefit. 'You did the pruning jolly well,' Lawrence confessed, ' I hope you'll live a long time, and barber up my novels for me before they're published.'

The finished book is a mélange of the perfectly realized and the inappropriately generalized, like so much of Lawrence's fiction. The day-by-day accounts of the life of the Morel family are sensitive, accurate, and fully convincing. Lawrence is never better than when he has his eye firmly fixed on an object. But when he lifts his head to consider, and to generalize, the prose is unrelentingly dead, and false. Consider this reflection on Paul Morel's predicament:

> He looked round. A good many of the nicest men he knew were like himself, bound in by their own virginity, which they could not break out of. They were so sensitive to their women, that they would go without them forever rather than do them a hurt, an injustice. Being the sons of mothers whose husbands had blundered rather brutally through their feminine sanctities, they were themselves too diffident and shy. For a woman was like their mother, and they were full of the sense of their mother.

This screams out to be quoted, and I will bet that if you find a used paperback of *Sons and Lovers*, this passage will have ink lines under it. The further that Lawrence moves from the particularities of his subject, the less successful he is likely to be, and the more likely an undergraduate is to underline the passage. In *Sons and Lovers*, there are no *other* 'nicest men' who are just like Paul. There may be some out there somewhere, but they never get a look in. Only Paul is just like Paul; when he is allowed to be, *Sons and Lovers* is a work of genius.

When it was published by Duckworth in 1913, reviews were generally adulatory, though a little concerned by Mr Lawrence's topics. *The Saturday Review* notice was typical, and a little equivocal: 'we know of no active English novelist – today – who has Mr Lawrence's power to put into words the rise and fall of the passions.' According to John Middleton Murry, Lawrence was now in the vanguard of the young novelists: 'emphatically the coming man. And his novels were, naturally, the pre-requisite of the most established reviewers.'

Lawrence was pleased by the attention but, having finished a work, he quickly moved on to the next. A novel was done when it went to the publishers – the internal business that it enacts finally incarnate on the printed page. But in the case of *Sons and Lovers*, there was a last, and not entirely congenial, duty: Garnett requested that he design the dustwrapper himself. Lawrence was a bit nonplussed. In those days, nobody thought much about dustwrappers, which were utilitarian things, usually lacking illustration, and frequently disposed of by the bookshop assistant at point of purchase. (This is, of course, why pre-1919 dust wrappers are so rare, and consequently so valuable.)

It was apparent, in giving Lawrence this brief, that his publisher saw it as a major selling point that the novel was an inside account of working-class life. (He can write books! He can even design dustwrappers!) Could he, they inquired, design a wrapper with a picture of a colliery on it? Exasperated, Lawrence pointed out that he was living on a lakeside in Italy, 'with no coal mines within miles and miles', and that in any case his artistic powers were not up to the task. He tried, failed, gave over the commission to his friend Ernest Collings, who couldn't do it either. Eventually Duckworth, curiously incapable of finding an illustrator who could draw a coal mine, produced the book in a typographic wrapper, with Lawrence's blurb on the front cover.

So the dustwrapper of *Sons and Lovers*, bearing the author's own précis of the novel, has something more than fetishistic value. But it still has plenty of that. A nice, crisp unwrapped copy of the book is probably worth £1,000 ($1,800) today. No wrappered one has appeared since that copy of Dennis Wheatley's (and mine) in 1979. It's hard to guess what one would fetch today, but with dustwrappered first editions of *The Great Gatsby* or *The Sun Also Rises* now breaking the £50,000 ($90,000) barrier, it is hard to see that *Sons and Lovers* would be worth much less.

Lawrence would be both amused and horrified. He cared nothing for first editions, and never read his books once they had been published. He disposed of the manuscript of *Sons and Lovers* by swapping it for a farm in New Mexico owned by his friend and patron Mabel Dodge Luhan (who later used it to pay for treatment by her psychoanalyst). Lawrence probably got the worst of the deal – by the time of the transaction, in 1924, it was an important manuscript, and the ranch was a pretty poor ranch. But he wouldn't have cared.

Lawrence makes the point, perfectly, in the essay 'The Bad Side of Books': 'Books to me are incorporate things, voices in the air . . . What do I care for first or last editions? I have never read one of my own published works. To me, no book has a date, no work has a binding.' In his Introduction to a bibliography of his work, published in 1924, he finds the right metaphor for this attitude: 'To every man who struggles with his own soul in mystery, a book that is a book flowers once, and seeds, and is gone. First editions or forty-first are only the husks of it.'

This makes one, as a dealer in such husks, feel sufficiently humbled. The content is what matters, the trappings merely a question of time and place. To an engaged reader, what does it matter what edition he may be reading? But I still wish I had my wrappered *Sons and Lovers* back. Alas, I sold it in my first catalogue, in 1982, for £1,850 ($3,300), an occasion doubly embarrassing in retrospect. First, I should have kept the damn thing (it's a bookseller's lament); but second, and more importantly, I was so taken by the rarity of it that I had a headline above my catalogue entry, which read: 'IN THE DUSTWRAPPER!' The capitals are, in retrospect, forgivable, but the exclamation point is not. Exclamation points are most frequently employed by people who use little hearts to dot their 'i's, and draw smiley faces. In the intervening twenty-two years I have never used one again in a catalogue. If the apocryphal brave little Spartan boy could remain impassive while a fox was chewing on his vitals, eschewing exclamation of any kind, then, I resolved, so should I.

THE CATCHER IN THE RYE

Notoriously reclusive, fiercely self-protective, skittish as a field mouse yet ornery as a polecat, J.D. Salinger is one of the contemporary writers least likely to be a congenial subject for a biographer. He has made few public appearances, granted almost no interviews, and his family and friends (who call him Jerry) are almost as jealous of his privacy as he is. Nobody knows much about him. Following the publication of *The Catcher in the Rye*, in 1951, he published three further books over the next twelve years, before withdrawing into seclusion in New Hampshire, where he is rumoured to have been scribbling away ever since.

Naturally enough, the more reclusive Salinger has become, the more fascinating he seems. *Catcher* is unquestionably one of the seminal post-war novels, and in Holden Caulfield, Salinger produced literature's first teenager, in the modern sense. Like D.H. Lawrence's protagonist in *Sons and Lovers*, Holden is sensitive, confused, passionate, and alienated from his surroundings. But unlike Paul Morel, he is gauche, smouldering, full of half-baked opinions, gratuitously disaffected. Lawrence's hero is a young *man* – it is impossible to imagine Paul Morel squeezing his pimples – whereas Holden is a recognizably new *category* of person. In only a few years, the type had assumed a kind of cultural centrality, most memorably portrayed by James Dean in *Rebel Without a Cause* (1955).

Small wonder, then, that the late Ian Hamilton, man-of-letters and stylish biographer of Robert Lowell, should have turned his sights on Salinger. Intelligent, waspish but sympathetic by nature, he may have assumed that Salinger would have seen in him an attractive prospective biographer. In 1985, he wrote to Salinger to ask if he would co-operate in his researches. Unlike most people who write to Salinger, he actually got an answer to his letter; like those few who do get replies, the reply was no. In fact, in uncharacteristically forthcoming mode, Salinger begged Hamilton to abandon the project and to leave him alone.

As we know, Hamilton persevered, publishing the excellent *In Search of J.D. Salinger* in 1988. The book had originally been entitled *J.D. Salinger: A Writing Life*, and had reached proof stage, when Salinger sued Hamilton, claiming that Hamilton's quotations from his letters to his friends (held at the Firestone Library, Princeton) constituted a breach of copyright. The case went to the Supreme Court of the State of New Jersey. Salinger won, the book was suppressed, and had to be entirely rewritten, without using the letters. (Copies of the suppressed proof are now worth £1,000 ($1,800).)

Throughout the case, and in spite of the fact that Hamilton was a friend of mine, my sympathies lay with Salinger. If he wanted to be the literary world's Greta Garbo, surely he had earned the right to be left alone? How curious it was, then, that at the very end of the affair, Salinger was threatening a further law suit, not against Hamilton, but against me. That was a little hurtful; Salinger doesn't even know me, and anyway *Catcher in the Rye* is one of my favourite books. I first read it in the middle 1950s, and the irritable and opinionated Holden Caulfield became one of my abiding role models.

I didn't know it then but Holden had made his first appearance, in 1941, in a short story about a boy who runs away from prep school. It was accepted by *The New Yorker* – the ultimate accolade at the time – but never printed (1941 was a bad year to encourage acts of desertion). Holden had a tenacious grasp on Salinger's imagination – he admitted that the character was a self-portrait, and a girlfriend from that time reported that Salinger referred to Holden as if he were a real person, and frequently quoted his opinions. The boy appeared, in various guises, in Salinger's stories throughout the 1940s, and two chapters of

Catcher were published as stories in magazines in 1945 and 1946.

It was an odd time to be writing with such intensity, because Salinger was also serving overseas, and was present at the Utah Beach landings in early June of 1944, with a gun in one hand and a pen in the other. A wartime colleague remembers him as different from the other soldiers: 'He didn't join in the drinking and card playing. Even during the hottest campaigns, he was writing, sending off to magazines.'

This concentration was a feature of Salinger's dedication from the very start: 'I won't say I'm a born writer, but I'm certainly a born professional. I don't think I ever *selected* writing as a profession. I just started to write when I was 18 or so and never stopped.' Even this single-mindedness took some knocks – he had a nervous breakdown at the end of the war – and he began to doubt his staying powers. 'I am a dash man, not a miler, and it is probable that I will never write a novel.' But he was admired and encouraged by other writers, who had followed his stories in *The New Yorker* and *Colliers*. When he met Hemingway in Paris at the Ritz, on Liberation Day in 1944, the two spent their time in mutual admiration. (Meeting Hemingway's biographer, a few years later, Salinger was disparaging about him, and intimated that the only great American writer since Melville was J.D. Salinger.)

Sustained by the praise and reinvigorated on his

return to New York, Salinger got back to work on the projected novel amidst the bustle of the city. Finding himself unable to concentrate with his usual compulsiveness, he soon decamped to Connecticut, shunning all company save that of his dog: 'You don't have to take time to explain to a dog, even in words of one syllable, that there are times when a man needs to be at his typewriter.'

Within the next year, he had a draft of the novel ready, and there were publishers queuing up. He had made a name for himself with his short stories, and even before publishing a novel was widely regarded as the most brilliant of young American writers. Robert Giroux, then an editor at Harcourt Brace, wrote to ask if he could publish a collection of the stories. 'No reply. Months later . . . a tall, sad-looking young man with a long face and deep-set black eyes walked in, saying, "It's not my stories that should be published first, but the novel I'm working on . . . about this kid in New York during the Christmas holidays."' In no time they had shaken hands on a deal, but to Salinger's disgust and Giroux's humiliation, the agreement was terminated by Giroux's boss, Eugene Reynal, who hated the book: 'Is Holden Caulfield supposed to be crazy?' he asked, scathingly, and stupidly. More than usually disgruntled, Salinger took the manuscript to Little, Brown, who accepted it immediately. But nothing they could do pleased their new author. Even

when he was told that the book had been picked as a
Book of the Month Club selection – guaranteeing large
sales – all he could focus on was whether this would
delay publication. He refused to allow proofs to go out
to reviewers, and objected violently to having a picture
of himself on the back of the dustwrapper. Dismayed,
his editor inquired, glacially, whether he wanted the
book published, or merely printed?

However you choose to describe it, the book was
issued on 16 July 1951, Salinger having taken himself
off to England for a couple of months to avoid having
to read reviews. He needn't have worried, most serious
reviewers loved the novel: *The New York Times* called it
'an unusually brilliant first novel, and *The Philadelphia
Enquirer* found its author 'a fresh and vigorous fiction
talent'. As you might expect, there were a few demur-
ring voices, mostly objecting to the book's frankness
of tone. *The Christian Science Monitor* thought it immoral
and perverse, and one assiduous lady reader counted,
in its 187 pages, 295 takings of the Lord's name in vain,
and an astonishing 587 blasphemies (or just over three
per page). Such reviews were, of course, good for sales:
the book was reprinted five times in July, three times
in August, and twice in September. It seemed impossible to print enough copies to satisfy the demand.

The Catcher in the Rye was published in England by
Hamish Hamilton in 1953, much to Salinger's pleasure,
though the reception was not as enthusiastic as in

America. Hamish Hamilton had feared this, and appended a cack-handed blurb to the English edition: 'Although the dialogue is distinctly American in vernacular and cadence, it is so masterly that English readers will not find it in the least difficult.' They didn't, but a surprising number of wearyingly superior reviewers found the book crass and boring – by implication, like most things American. The tone of *Punch*'s reviewer was characteristic. *Catcher* was damned as sentimental – though this, the writer admitted, 'may merely be the reaction of a corrupt European who prefers a soft surface and a hard core'.

But it didn't matter if the English wanted to sniff. By 1953 *Catcher* was already a huge success. It had reached number 4 in *The New York Times* bestseller list in 1951, and had steady and escalating sales in the next decade. By 1961 it was selling a remarkable 125,000 copies a year, and today annual sales are more than twice that figure.

Salinger was initially heartened by the response but the pleasure soon wore off: 'most of it I found hectic and professionally and personally demoralising. Let's say I'm getting good and sick of bumping into that blown-up photograph of my face on the back of the dust jacket. I look forward to the day when I see it flapping against a lamp-post in a cold, wet Lexington Avenue wind . . .' From the third edition onwards, Salinger's picture no longer appeared on the jacket. It made him look a little unfriendly, which he was, but it also rendered him recognizable, which he had absolutely no desire to be. He wished to be left alone with his dog and his typewriter.

No wonder, then, that he didn't welcome Ian Hamilton's letter all those years later. He didn't want to be written about, analysed and disclosed. The publication of the biography distressed him considerably. Unsurprisingly, the affair also left a sour taste in Hamilton's mouth. In 1989 he suggested I buy the archive of papers relating to the book: correspondence, tapes and transcripts of interviews, notes, manuscripts, court papers: the lot. Certain that some university library would have an interest – the case was a famous one – I agreed the deal, and offered the material to the manuscripts librarian of an American university. He bought it immediately, and it was shipped off within a few days.

It was only six days later that I got a frantic phone call from America, to say that the archive had arrived at almost the same instant as a letter from J.D. Salinger's lawyers, demanding the return of all of the material relating to the law suit with Hamilton.

'What are you going to do?' I asked, a little anxiously.

'Send it all back to you immediately,' he said firmly, which was nice of him.

No sooner had the material arrived, than I received

a phone call from the offices of Salinger's literary agents, Harold Ober Associates. I was informed by a woman with a voice racked by indignation and cigarettes, which could have frozen the blood of an Orc, that I was in serious trouble. Mr Salinger's lawyers were on to me. I was in contempt of the Supreme Court of the State of New Jersey.

I was rather sad, and distinctly surprised, to hear it. I've never lived in the state of New Jersey, and though I've always rather disapproved of it, it would be an exaggeration to say that I hold it (much less its Supreme Court) in contempt. But it seems that, amongst Ian Hamilton's court papers, was a copy of a deposition given by Salinger, a document of some 200 plus pages, in which he described to the court his objections to the biography, and his own methods of writing and conducting himself in the world. This document, like the other depositions in the case, had been placed 'under seal', which means it cannot be made public in any way.

Mr Salinger had a whole army of lawyers. They wrote to me, faxed me, rang me with a total disregard for the time differences between New York and London. A long consultation with Ian Hamilton's solicitor confirmed, sadly, that the American lawyers were right – that the legal material was never Ian's to sell.

On the other hand, I had bought it in good faith, and it wasn't clear that this particular American law could be enforced against me in England: a point I made forcibly to my antagonists. They agreed that it might be difficult pursuing me. Instead, they said, they would impound Mr Hamilton's American earnings, and make sure that, the next time he tried to enter America, he was tossed in jail. I conveyed the news to Ian, who took it with surprising equanimity, and said that I should do whatever I wanted. But it was clear the game was up. I proposed a compromise to Salinger's agent, the one with the battle-axe voice.

'It seems to me,' I said, 'that I haven't knowingly done anything wrong. And I stand to lose money if I return the deposition.'

'Yeah, yeah,' she said, grudgingly.

'I am an admirer of Mr Salinger's, and I have no desire to cause him distress . . .'

'Uh huh . . .'

'So I would suggest that I send you back the deposition, and in acknowledgement, that Mr Salinger inscribe for me my first edition copy of *Catcher in the Rye.*' Salinger, as you may suppose, is a notoriously parsimonious inscriber; I've only ever seen two inscribed first editions of *Catcher*, the lesser of which is worth £30,000 ($54,000).

There was an ominous silence on the line.

'Hello?' I said.

'That's blackmail!' shrieked the voice from Hell.

'On the contrary,' I explained reasonably, 'it seems

to me it would be a perfect, indeed a gentlemanly, acknowledgement on his part of a bit of fair-minded behaviour on my part . . .'

There was a loud barking noise, as if the literary agent had been replaced by an asthmatic seal.

'Surely,' I continued, 'this is the right result? Mr Salinger gets his material returned, and I get a little memento for my bookshelf.'

There was a further, longer, and yet more sinister, silence.

'I'll send it back tomorrow,' I said, and I did. In my business, you have to know when you're licked. Anyway, I soon sold Salinger's original letter to Hamilton to a New York collector, and the residue of the archive to the Firestone Library, at a reasonable profit.

But there is still an empty space on my bookshelves where that inscribed *Catcher in the Rye* should be resting. 'For Rick,' I imagine that it would have read, 'with the grudging compliments of Jerry Salinger.'

SEVEN PILLARS OF
WISDOM

I don't like to use the word sumptuous about books –
it seems more applicable to sofas – but if there is a
sumptuous twentieth-century book, then this is it. It's
lavishly bound, fat and comfortable, with high-quality
setting of the text in Caslon type, and superbly and
copiously illustrated by many of the leading artists of
the period: Colin Gill, Eric Kennington, Henry Lamb,
William Roberts, Edward Wadsworth, Frank Dobson,
Augustus John, John Singer Sargent, Gertrude
Hermes, Gilbert Spencer, William Rothenstein, Paul
Nash. It's a magisterial object, which demands to be
looked at, stroked and weighed, contemplated inside
and out, like a bibliographic work of art. It is less easy
to read, but *reading,* its very appearance seems to
proclaim, is hardly the point.

It's gorgeous, if slightly overdressed, and it was only
available if you subscribed to buy one of the 170 copies,
for thirty guineas, the equivalent today of about £1,200

($2,200). Lawrence intended a 'titanic' book – not, presumably, because it was so heavy it would sink – and did produce a masterpiece, though ironically not for its text, but for the superb quality of its production. Everyone has heard of it, though only two people of my acquaintance have read it, not because it is difficult (like *Finnegans Wake*) but because it is boring. Listen to this description of the Arabs:

> as unstable as water, and like water would perhaps finally prevail. Since the dawn of life, in successive waves they had been dashing themselves against the coasts of flesh. Each wave was broken, but, like the sea, wore away ever so little of the granite on which it failed . . . and some day, ages yet, might roll unchecked over the place where the material world had been, and God would move upon the face of those waters. One such wave I raised and rolled before the breath of an idea, til it reached its crest, and toppled and fell at Damascus. The wash of that wave, thrown back by the resistance of vested things, will provide the matter of the following wave, when in fullness of time the sea shall be raised once more.

It's easy selectively to quote the unfortunate passages in even the best of books, but this unhappily sustained metaphor is typical: typical because it is a recurrent fault in Lawrence's prose and typical, too, because the passage ends with a bit of barely disguised self-aggrandisement. For the text is actually little more than an account, much of it baldly untruthful, of what Lawrence 'tried to do in Arabia', and of how gloriously he would have succeeded, had not the forces of age and conservatism thwarted him. As an exercise in self-mythologizing the book was to become an unparalleled success.

The title was inspired by Proverbs 9:1: 'Wisdom hath filled a house, she hath hewn out her Seven Pillars', to which the author characteristically appended the subtitle: *A Triumph*. Self-published by T. E. Lawrence in 1926, *Seven Pillars* is one of the rarest, most striking, and most valuable books of twentieth-century literature. So assiduously is it sought after – copies come on the market at most once or twice a year – that in the 1980s, the late Harry Spiro, a rich and manically acquisitive New York collector seemed intent on cornering the market. He began by paying something like £4,000 ($7,200) a copy, which rose and rose, and still he bought and bought, until sometime in the middle nineties, he decided he had had enough. By then he owned more than a dozen copies. With the books now fetching up to £35,000 ($63,000), he presumably had not so much a smile as a wolfish grin on his face.

And yet it could be argued that his multiple copies of *Seven Pillars* are not true first editions. The history of the text is absorbing. Lawrence wrote the first draft in 1919, when it was lost, or stolen from him, at Reading railway station in November. Disconsolate, but encouraged by his friends, Lawrence undertook to rewrite the text, which was completed the next May. Unsatisfied by this draft, which he disparagingly called 'My Boy-Scout book', he started again, finishing in 1922.

He had learned the hard way the unwisdom of having only one copy of his manuscript. He was contemplating commissioning a typescript with carbon-copies, the usual procedure, when he learned that, for only a slightly larger outlay, he could have the book hand-set by the compositors of the *Oxford Times*. Copies were printed on thin, poor quality proofing paper, to circulate to his friends for comment. He was anxious lest his work be stolen by a rogue typographer, who might be tempted to publish it under his own name, and later, perhaps, become known as 'Fred Muggins of Arabia'. So Lawrence cannily submitted the chapters in random unnumbered order, and never divulged the title of the book, which he later supplied in typescript himself. I'll bet that fooled them.

In the autumn of 1922, he hand-corrected the inevitable printer's errors, had the copies bound, and circulated them to a group of friends who included Robert Graves, E.M. Forster, Thomas Hardy, Bernard Shaw, Rudyard Kipling, and D.G. Hogarth (Keeper of the Ashmolean Museum). Within a few months, when Lady Scott inquired if she might borrow a copy, Lawrence replied, sadly, that he didn't have one to lend:

> You want a copy! Unfortunately so do I. Of the six copies which exist only one has ever been returned by a borrower: and that copy was foolishly lent a second time, and hasn't come back. So as a fact I want six copies.

He was encouraged by the enthusiasm of his readers. Siegfried Sassoon wrote:

> it is a GREAT BOOK, blast you . . . And thank all gods, heathen deities, fetiches, Theocracies, inter- cessors, and Emmanuels for a man who writes a good book and doesn't sell it for his soul to a pimp of a publisher!

Lawrence was soon contemplating production of a lavish, privately published, edition. But what, exactly, was the 'book' that was to be published? He consid- ered publication of the corrected 1922 text, but wondered if it should be radically abridged from its extraordinarily inflated 300,000 words. He was worried, too, about the quality of his writing, and reread his draft of the book in despair. Leafing through their letters, he noticed that though his first readers had praised the book, few of them had been enthusiastic about its prose. E.M. Forster proffered some stylistic analysis:

> The criticism I'd offer is that your reflective style is not properly under control. Almost at once, when you describe your thoughts, you become obscure, and the slightly strained sense which you then. . . lend words, does not bring your sentences the richness you intended, imparts not colour but gumminess.

Gumminess? That's absolutely right, and entirely damning, however neatly phrased. Lawrence was grateful for the advice, but incapable of profiting from it. The finished version is unrelentingly verbose, if blessedly shorter.

He was fortunate in his friends. Another of them, Edward Garnett, discoverer of Conrad and editor of *Sons and Lovers*, offered to abridge the text on Lawrence's behalf, and produced a draft which cut it by half. Lawrence wasn't entirely convinced:

> What am I to do? Publish the Garnett abridgement after all . . . and use its profits to publish a limited illustrated complete edition . . . publish nothing . . . print privately? Hardy read the thing lately and made me very proud with what he said of it. Shaw praised it . . .

The final text was eventually abridged by Lawrence himself, following Forster's advice. He wrote to Mrs Thomas Hardy (who preferred the longer version) that 'the little cut out was all redundant stuff: mostly super-fluous adjectives.' In fact, 170 pages had been excised, which represents about 70,000 adjectives.

Plans for a Subscribers' Edition were eventually settled. Friends were requested to find subscribers who would pay thirty guineas in advance for one of 100 projected copies. First soundings were discouraging: only thirty-seven possible buyers emerged, and Lawrence was finding that the task of revising the text, and organizing its production, was sapping what little energy he had left over from his duties with the Tank Corps. And money – as any publisher of fine books would have predicted – was running out. Costs had first been projected at something over £3,000 ($5,400), which, given only 100 subscribers, would have made the book break even, for Lawrence thought it improper that he should profit personally from a book that recounted his war-time experiences. But breaking even soon looked an impossibly optimistic goal, instead of a noble sacrifice.

Two years went by. The pages of the book were laboriously set, and reset, by the compositors, until they eventually met Lawrence's high standards. Bindings were commissioned. The illustrations were finalized. Subscriptions mounted. So did costs. When copies were eventually sent out to the 170 subscribers, Lawrence reckoned that the production cost of each book was something over £90 ($160) a volume. He was losing money hand over fist.

He made up some of the difference by borrowing money, and selling his Fourth Folio Shakespeare. But it wasn't enough, and debts mounted. Eventually, he was forced to reconsider his antipathy to a trade edition of the book, even if it came after publication of the Subscribers' Edition. He had always been adamant that he ought to 'avoid the notoriety of being on sale in England'. But reluctantly he agreed in 1927 that Cape could publish an abridgement of the book, *Revolt in the Desert*. Debts were cleared in a few weeks, and Lawrence rather enjoyed the notoriety.

It had been a Herculean undertaking, and after many doubts and innumerable crises, Lawrence was pleased with his Subscribers' Edition: 'unless I am wrong,' he said, 'it will be celebrated one day.' The 170 copies sold out, though they were admired more for the opulence of their production than for their contents.

The Subscribers' Edition of *Seven Pillars* is, ultimately, a triumph of form over content. Yet my friend Edward Maggs, whose firm Maggs Brothers are the most experienced dealers in T.E. Lawrence material, maintains that its gumminess is no reason to withdraw one's admiration. 'Of course it is a failure,' he maintains stoutly, 'but it is an heroic failure.' I don't have any problems with that, and it's generous of Ed, but it sure doesn't make me want to read the book. I'd rather read a heroic success.

So here is the question that you may be asking yourself: if one of the 170 copies of the 1926 *Seven Pillars* is now worth £35,000 ($63,000), how much is one of the six known copies of the 1922 Oxford edition worth? Nobody knew the answer to this – only two of the copies are in private hands, and none had ever appeared on the open market – until Tuesday, 22 May 2001, when Lawrence's own copy, Number 1, came under the hammer at Christie's, New York. It sold for £700,000 ($1.26 million), which was more than four times the price ever fetched for a twentieth-century book.

In twenty years of dealing rare modern books, I have never owned a copy of the 1926 *Seven Pillars*. It's one of my blind spots. Not only *Seven Pillars*, but Lawrence generally. I'm usually pretty attentive about the details of bibliographies and values, but virtually nothing of Lawrence's will stick in my mind. I'm not interested.

This is not an uncommon condition, according to Lawrence's biographer Jeremy Wilson, who observes that 'the public no longer knows what should be believed and what should be denied and, as a result, many serious-minded people have come to regard the subject of T.E. Lawrence with caution, if not distaste.'

The only adequate remedy for this, by implication, is to read his 1,188-page biography of Lawrence. But if you have decided that you are not interested in Lawrence, you are unlikely to do so much reading.

I have the same problem with the work of Winston Churchill, though I did recently read Roy Jenkins' biography, which left me with immense admiration for Churchill, about whom I had been reprehensibly ignorant. But I still don't want to stock his books: he may be surpassingly admirable, but I don't feel comfortable with the sort of people who collect his works. I feel the same way about Lawrence (except for the admiration).

Collectors are an odd lot, both obsessional and compulsive, secretive and retentive. Usually they collect the books of authors whom they enjoy reading, and value them accordingly, and harmlessly. But Lawrence and Churchill collectors are different, there is something edgy and personal about their project, something (as Dame Edna might say) spooky. I don't believe that, in their dreams, they are swanning about on camels, or directing the Second World War. Rather, that their sense of self is fuelled by their association with a hero through whom they feel enlarged. (Jung calls this identification with an archetype 'psychic inflation'.)

'Now old Winston,' you can imagine such collectors musing, 'he was my sort of man!' Who are the major collectors of Churchill? The Sultan of Brunei, newspaper magnate Conrad Black, American Presidential candidate Steve Forbes. Show me a book-collecting captain-of-industry type, and I'll bet you he collects Churchill, or Roosevelt, or (God help us) Napoleon.

Lawrence collectors aren't quite so grand, but then again neither was Lawrence. I've happily avoided them, and him, for most of my dealing life, and my major engagement with Lawrenciana was an inadvertent one.

Some few years ago, I purchased rather a bad painting by Wyndham Lewis, on whom I was keen at the time. Painted in 1935, it depicted an ill-painted desert scene with some hills in the background and a white-caped man riding a horse. The horse was rendered in the Vorticist manner, which only succeeded in making it cock-eyed, and as if it was about to fall over.

I put the painting up in my shop, where it met with universal derision. Even I had begun to hate it, when one day a T.E. Lawrence collector walked into the shop, on one of his infrequent visits from New York. He looked over at the picture. 'Is that new?' he demanded aggressively. 'Why didn't you offer it to me!'

'Sure, because it's Lawrence of bloody Arabia, right?' I answered.

'I know it is,' he said. 'How much is it?'

It was marked at £5,500 ($10,000) because, however nasty it was, it was after all an oil by Wyndham Lewis. But *now* it was a picture of T.E. Lawrence by Lewis. My customer informed me that Lewis had been given £50 ($90) to produce one of the illustrations for *Seven Pillars*, and had failed to deliver on time. This was either a later version of the picture, he told me smugly, or some post-dated study for it. It was probably worth £20,000 ($36,000), if you had the sense – like him, and unlike me – to know what it was.

He didn't even demand a discount, which was rare, and bought it at the marked price of £5,500. Then he insisted that I buy him lunch at The Ivy, which is my favourite restaurant, for having been so stupid.

I didn't enjoy it much.

THE COLOSSUS

You can't afford to be sentimental as a rare book dealer, or to form attachments that are too intense. Unless you have a lot of money, the books that come through your hands aren't for keeping, however much you may love them. 'Love', of course, is a provocative word here, and I use it hesitantly. But every now and again a book pops up that has such a visceral appeal that you feel a resolute attachment to it, almost erotic, and you don't wish to let it go. This capacity of the occasional volume to transmit a force-field of attraction, nicely described by Jeanette Winterson as 'the psychometry of books', can affect me more deeply and more permanently than many of the people I meet. I remember, for instance, only a small percentage of the students I taught at the University of Warwick. Equally, I can recall a similarly small number of the books that have passed through my hands. But the implication is clear: some of the best books have been more memorable than the bulk of the people.

I am unembarrassed by this. I suppose you could argue the question in principle, but take the following instance instead, from my Catalogue 16, issued in 1992.

PLATH, SYLVIA. *The Colossus and Other Poems*, New York, 1962. First American edition. The dedication copy, inscribed by Plath: FOR TED 'Of Whom Colossus and Prince Otto learn their craft and art with love Sylvia.'

If you don't immediately feel how exciting this book is – if you haven't, in some form or another, just whispered 'that is so fabulous!' to yourself – I'm afraid you don't have the makings of a book collector. I'm not even sure if I would like you very much. As I remarked in my catalogue note, it's an exceedingly resonant inscription. The reference, of course, is to Sylvia's German-American father Otto Plath, who died when she was only eight, and with whom she was obsessed throughout her life. He dominated her imagination, and all of the men in her life successively fell under his shadow.

Sylvia and Ted used to play with a Ouija board, when, according to Ted:

'spirits' would regularly arrive with instructions for her from one Prince Otto . . . When she pressed for a more personal communication, she would be told that Prince Otto could not speak to her directly, because he was under orders from The Colossus . . . her effort to come to terms with the meaning this Colossus held for her, in her poetry, became more and more central as the years passed.

So it is difficult to imagine a more intimate inscription on Plath's first book: to her adored husband, Ted Hughes, with references to her Olympian father, and his guiding spirit. Ted and Otto are shockingly conjoined in her most famous poem, 'Daddy', with its dark evocation of her remote, powerful, father:

> I have always been scared of *you*
> With your Luftwaffe, your gobbledygoo.
> And your neat moustache
> And your Aryan eye, bright blue,
> Panzer-man, panzer-man O You –

Otto Plath's death was the defining event of Sylvia's life, from which moment abiding happiness became unattainable for her. Her attempted suicide, at the age of twenty (the subject of her only novel, *The Bell Jar*) was intended, she recalled, to reunite her with her dead father. And so ineradicable was her attachment, not to Otto's memory but to his abiding internal presence, that she seemed destined to project his figure onto her future lovers. As 'Daddy' continues, the figures of Prince Otto and Ted Hughes become indistinguishable:

> I made a model of you,
> A man in black with a Meinkampf look
>
> And a love of the rack and the screw.
> And I said I do, I do.

And the poem ends with the (unrealistic) hope that the presence, both empowering and inhibiting, of the dead father has been blotted out by the coming of the new love:

> There's a stake in your fat black heart
> And the villagers never liked you.
> They are dancing and stamping on you.
> They always *knew* it was you.
> Daddy, daddy, you bastard, I'm through.

This is chillingly unforgettable, its author the very model of the neurotic, passionately intense girl that mothers warn their sons against. When Ted and Sylvia first met at a Cambridge party in February 1956, the mutual attraction was shocking to both of them. She kissed and bit him so hard that he bled.

They married four months later – 'Ted is the ideal, the one possible person,' she wrote – spent some time in America, then set up home in London, writing. Sylvia placed occasional poems in good magazines, but was frustrated in her attempts to get a book accepted. Ted's first book, *The Hawk in the Rain* was published by Faber in 1957. They lived in a hothouse of literary composition; she was thrilled for him, but envious. Relations were delicately poised, at once supportive and competitive, stimulating but potentially explosive. Sylvia worried about it: her journal entry of 7 November 1959 notes: 'Dangerous to be so close to Ted day in day out. I have no life separate from his, am likely to become a mere accessory . . . I must have a life that supports me inside.'

At Christmas, she put together fifty of her poems, and typed up the manuscript of *The Colossus and Other Poems*, which she submitted to Heinemann, at the request of the editor James Michie, who had admired her work in the *London Magazine*. A contract was signed, and the book dedicated to Ted – 'that paragon who has encouraged me through all my glooms about it.' When the book came out, some months later, she was disappointed to find a couple of misprints, but was 'delighted with the color of the cover . . . It is a nice fat book which takes up 3/4 of an inch on the shelf.' *(The Hawk in the Rain* was slimmer). 'I think they did a handsome job of it.'

The euphoria didn't last long. Reviews were complimentary, but Plath wasn't satisfied. Having yearned so poignantly to get a book into print, she was now unhappy because it didn't get more and better notices, win any prizes, make any money, or find an American publisher. Such is the pathology of ambition: a goal having been attained is merely redefined. Not enough to publish what was immediately hailed as an important book, it ought to have been a celebrated one. She was admired by a literate coterie, but now she wanted to be famous.

In May of the next year, Alfred Knopf agreed to publish *The Colossus* in America, though in a shortened version. The poet Marianne Moore had recommended dropping ten of the poems, and shortening and re-titling others. Sylvia acceded happily: 'It will be like a new book coming out,' she enthused, 'the one, the Ideal.' (The phrase, eerily, echoes her earlier description of Ted: presumably both were Platonic incarnations of perfection.) And, sure enough, reviews were extremely enthusiastic. Joyce Carol Oates, in *The New York Times*, expressed the prevalent feeling perfectly:

[Her poems] have that exquisite, heart-breaking quality about them that has made Sylvia Plath our acknowledged Queen of Sorrows, the spokeswoman for our most private, most helpless nightmares . . . Her poetry is as deathly as it is impeccable; it enchants us almost as powerfully as it must have enchanted her.

Instability, and the perceived imminence of ever-renewing crises, were essential components of Plath's nature, and art. *The Colossus and Other Poems* was published in America on Monday, 14 May 1962. On Friday of the same week, David and Assia Wevill – tenants at the Hughes's London flat – came to visit the couple in Devon. The evening went badly, and there are different accounts of what went wrong. It seems as if the attraction between Ted and Assia was palpable, and that Sylvia, naturally enough, reacted to it. Assia was later to maintain that had Sylvia not responded so strongly, it was unlikely that her later affair with Ted would have developed, which sounds both false and foolish.

Within a couple of months, Sylvia was all but consumed with jealous rage. In mid-July, when Ted was in London (visiting Assia?) Sylvia burned all of his papers that she could find – clearly the worst thing one can do to a writer, and the second time that Sylvia had done so. As the pages burned, Sylvia stoked through the ashes, and 'a name with black edges' unfurled itself: 'ASSIA'.

By September Ted had moved out. The marriage was over, and Sylvia, left with two little children, was inconsolable but not unproductive. As a poet she thrived on desolation, even as it devoured her. In the last weeks of her life she composed many of the great poems of her posthumous collection, *Ariel* (1965). This frenzy of composition was cathartic, and final: on the night of 11 February 1963, Sylvia carefully sealed the bedroom in which the babies were sleeping, and turned on the gas in the kitchen of her flat in Fitzroy Road. She was found dead the next morning. (Six years later, Assia Wevill killed both herself and her daughter by Hughes, Shura.)

Things had fallen apart almost as quickly as they had been put together. Only seven months after the loving, if ominous, inscription on that copy of *The Colossus*, Sylvia Plath, estranged from her husband, was dead. It would be consoling to hope that she had rejoined Prince Otto, but I rather doubt it. Rather, she became an icon for a generation of American feminists who regarded themselves as unconscionably disenfranchised, and whom Sylvia would have disliked. She came to be treated as if she were a spokeswoman for women's rights. But she was no such thing: she was far too self-absorbed to represent anyone but herself. And for that we can be nothing but grateful.

You may have been wondering – if not, you should have – how, since Ted Hughes was still vibrantly alive in 1992, that inscribed *Colossus* came on to the market? The answer was that he sold it. Like many authors, Hughes was unsentimental about the flotsam and jetsam of the world of letters, the various forms that paper can take: manuscripts, proofs, letters, inscribed books. He kept such things (his archive was eventually sold to Emory University), but he didn't make fetishes of them. The inscribed *Colossus*, which to many of us seems a magical object, was presumably, to him, just one of a number of books given to him by his ex-wife. That, *and* a form of money.

I was offered it, for £4,000 ($7,200), through Roy Davids, the Head of the Books and Manuscripts Department at Sotheby's, a friend of Ted's who occasionally acted as his agent. I bought it without hesitation, thinking only (a) that it was wonderful, and (b) that it must be worth more than *that*. After some time in its company, as my attachment to it increased, I catalogued it for £9,500 ($17,000).

No sooner had the catalogue come out, than I had a phone call from Roy Davids.

'Ted is furious!' he said.

It was obvious what he was referring to. 'Why's that?'

'He thinks dealers should only get 10 per cent,' said Roy, who knew better.

'Then you should explain to him that we often have to give discounts when we sell books, that cataloguing costs a lot, and that sometimes books don't sell. He's used to dealing with auctioneers, who never have to put up their own money, and who charge both the buyer and the seller.'

'I've explained that,' said Roy laconically, his tone indicating that Ted didn't buy a word of it. And in the meantime, I pointed out, Ted had his money (the amount he had asked for) and I only had an unsold book.

I wasn't surprised to get this reaction from Hughes, with whom I'd had tricky dealings in the past. I had previously catalogued a copy of *The Great Gatsby*, heavily annotated by Sylvia, which Ted later claimed 'had been stolen from [their home] Court Green'. I gave it back, though subsequent research established that it had been taken (not stolen, I presume) by Sylvia's mother. Ted returned it, grudgingly. He was a complex and difficult person, who did not wear his charisma lightly. His powers were withheld and distilled, and he positively throbbed with internal energy. It felt distinctly uncomfortable when he aimed it at you.

I can't recall cataloguing an item that was so widely remarked upon as that *Colossus*, and so greatly admired. There was even a correspondence about it in *The Times*, initiated by a former friend of Sylvia's, who argued that such an object ought not to be allowed to leave our shores. (And, by implication, that Ted should never have sold it.) I had no opinion about the latter charge, save that he owned the book, and it was his to sell. But why an American edition of a book, inscribed to her husband by an American poet, should be regarded as part of England's cultural heritage was obscure to me.

But however controversial, and however admired, the book failed to find a buyer. Maybe, in 1992, it was a little bit ahead of its time. Or perhaps my price was, for the Plath-Hughes industry was still in the process of construction. *The Colossus* sat on my shelves for many months, and though I did not cease to feel its power, I got increasingly irritated by it. The fact that it didn't sell began to undermine its desirability, even to me.

Late that year, I sold it to a canny and discriminating poetry collector from Philadelphia. He had always maintained that it was too expensive, and tabled an offer of $9,000 (£5,000) for it. Eventually, exasperatedly, I took it. He got a great book. It was sold a few years later, when he disposed of his collection, for a good deal more than my original price. Nowadays it is hard to say what it is worth, but I'd be happy to pay £25,000 ($45,000), and then try to figure it out.

No sooner had the book left my office, though, than it regained its former power. I missed it immediately, and I still do. The only small recompense was that I was able to report my reduced price to Roy Davids, to transmit to Ted as evidence that my original argument had been a fair one. Roy suggested that I forget about it (which was good advice), but did bring the matter up when he next visited Ted in Devon. Apparently he wasn't very impressed.

A CONFEDERACY
OF DUNCES

The tragedy is that John Kennedy Toole never knew he was John Kennedy Toole. I do not mean that he was some sort of foundling or psychotic. I mean it in the same sense that Vincent Van Gogh never knew he was Vincent Van Gogh – that his name would one day be conjured with, and revered. But compared to Toole, even the unhappy Van Gogh had a productive career. Though he only sold one picture in his life-time, he produced a compelling body of work, and had reason to believe that his time might come.

Ken Toole, as he was known, is the author of the acclaimed comic novel *A Confederacy of Dunces*, and one of a surprising number of Southern novelists – Margaret Mitchell and Harper Lee come immediately to mind – who wrote only one, important novel. Mitchell and Lee had the good sense to quit while they were ahead, as if in recognition of the sad fact that most novelists get worse. But Toole never even got to see his book in print.

Unable to find a publisher for what he considered a masterpiece, its author grew more and more despondent, and committed suicide in 1969. How the novel eventually found its way into print is one of the most interesting, tragic, and (belatedly) heartening, stories of publication history in the twentieth century.

Toole's protagonist, Ignatius J. Reilly of New Orleans, is an egregiously disgusting, loathsomely fat momma's boy, given to volcanic eructations, pompous and irascible. Armed with his MA in Medieval Studies, he is a fantasist claiming to be disgusted by everything the twentieth century has to offer: television, new cars, frozen food, hair spray, lanolin, cellophane, plastic, subdivisions, dacron and nylon, easy sex, democracy. In fact, though, he is devoted to comic books and going to the movies, and is one of the great consumers of fast food of all time. Stuffed with hot dogs and opinions, no character in literature is so comprehensively full of shit as Ignatius J. Reilly. Blubbery and repulsive, he hardly seems human: as if you had crossed W.C. Fields with a hippopotamus.

Nor is he, as many critics have claimed, an antihero. He is no sort of hero at all, and it is a considerable part of the book's genius that, centred so intently as it is on Ignatius, the reader rarely feels the smallest twinge of sympathy for its protagonist. That's hard to do: in general, to know someone thoroughly is to share and to understand their feelings, a process that seems inevitably to lead to sympathy. Even Raskolnikov, in *Crime and Punishment*, quivering with terror behind the door of the apartment in which he has just butchered Alyona Ivanovna and her half-sister, elicits a shameful compassion on the reader's part. It is easy to share another's terror. But the smugness and indolent delusions of Ignatius are totally, if comically, repellent.

It is only at the very end of the novel, in a brilliant reversal, that Toole makes us applaud Ignatius's final escape just as the ambulance rolls up to take him away to 'The Charity' mental hospital. Disgusting though he is, we finally prefer him in his unimproved version: 'Psychiatry is worse than communism. I refuse to be brainwashed. I won't be a robot!' Good for you! we say, rather surprised to hear ourselves saying it.

Toole may only be remembered for this one, great posthumous novel, but he compiled a surprising body of unpublished early work. In 1954, at the age of sixteen, he wrote *The Neon Bible*, a novel which he later described as 'a grim, adolescent sociological attack upon the hatreds spawned by the various Calvinist religions in the South'. He had the confidence to send the book off for publication, but it was rightly rejected. (Inevitably, it was published by Grove Press after Toole's apotheosis.) This was followed by a number of stories and poems – 'pieces and beginnings that were never inflicted on any editor'. After graduating from Tulane, Toole did an MA in English at Columbia, and taught for a short time at Hunter College, while starting his PhD.

In 1961 he was drafted, and sent by the Army to Puerto Rico to teach English to new recruits. It was the best thing that could have happened to him: his duties were risibly undemanding, and he had a room of his own, a desk and a typewriter. He spent the two years working on the novel *Humphrey Wilding*, which was to become *A Confederacy of Dunces*.

This change of title was inspired, and ironically prescient, citing lines from Swift: 'When a true genius appears in the world, you may know him by this sign, that the dunces are all in confederacy against him.' A brilliant title for a Southern work of satire. A perfect encapsulation of Ignatius J. Reilly's view of himself. But most significantly a maxim applied more appropriately to the book's author than to its protagonist. It would be overstating the case to say that the publishing dunces ganged up on John Kennedy Toole, but they wouldn't publish his book. And that was seriously stupid of them.

Sadly, the chief of these dunces was the otherwise estimable Robert Gottlieb, the senior editor at Simon & Schuster. Toole found himself unable to work after the assassination of President Kennedy in November of 1963 – 'I couldn't write anymore. Nothing seemed funny to me' – and so sent the manuscript to Simon & Schuster because they had published his favourite novel, Bruce Jay Friedman's *Stern*. Though Toole did not know anything about him, Gottlieb should have been just the man for the job. An editor of great energy and sympathy, he had a good eye for a promising manuscript, and the patience to work with an author to nurse it into shape. It was Gottlieb, after all, who had persuaded Joseph Heller to carry on with *Catch-22*.

Gottlieb liked *A Confederacy of Dunces*, but he didn't like it enough. It was funny, some of the characters were perfectly drawn, and a few episodes were explosively amusing. But, he told Toole, there was one great flaw: it wasn't clear what the book, funny as it was, *was about.* 'In other words, there must be a point to everything you have in the book, a real point, not just amusingness that's forced to figure itself out.' But he was anxious, he stressed, to work with Toole on the manuscript.

At first, Toole was heartened by the response, which if it wasn't an outright acceptance, wasn't quite a rejection either. But even after he had made substantial revisions to the text, and resubmitted the manuscript, Gottlieb still wasn't satisfied: 'with all its wonderfulnesses, the book – even better plotted (and still better plotable) – does not have a reason; it's a brilliant exercise in invention, but unlike *CATCH* [22] and *MOTHER'S KISSES* and *V* and the others, it isn't really *about* anything. And that's something no one can do anything about. Certainly an editor can't say: "put meaning in."'

Gottlieb nowhere describes, in this short correspondence, exactly what he means by 'meaning'. I do not observe this by way of philosophical cavil. Put it this way: reading *Confederacy*, a roiling satire on the South and on modern life, and a terrifically funny story, is undeniably delightful. What is it, then, that is missing? A moral? Surely not. I suspect that what Gottlieb was looking for was more coherence, in the Aristotelian sense: that one incident should follow another because it is probable that it would do so. Whereas *Confederacy* (like *Don Quixote*) moves from incident to incident not in the sense that one follows from, or causes, the other, but because each absurdly reveals Ignatius in his downward slide towards freedom. And that may not have been good enough for Gottlieb, but it has been wonderful for millions of readers since then.

It isn't clear, during this exasperating two-year process of revising, corresponding about, and reformulating *Confederacy*, whether Toole was regularly submitting the text to other publishers, and if so, which. It was apparently turned down by Knopf (where, ironically, Gottlieb later moved), and, legend has it, a legion of others, but no one knows the details. Toole accepted that the text had its flaws: it was that little bit picaresque, perhaps there was too much of Ignatius, certainly the characters of the Levys and Myrna didn't come alive. He vowed to try again, though he began joking to friends that he would be 'an old, toothless man' by the time the book was published.

In fact he was increasingly despondent, and eventually asked for his manuscript to be returned. There is 'something of my soul in the thing', he said. 'I can't let it rot without my trying.' This is both an admirable and a dangerous sentiment. On 26 March 1969, he drove out to a deserted spot in the country, put a hose pipe into his car exhaust and stuck the other end through the window. He was thirty-one years old.

Toole always insisted that Ignatius was neither a self-portrait nor an alter ego, but he does bear some similarities to Toole's mother, Thelma. Mrs Toole was peculiar to look at, eccentric, aggressive, and insistently self-regarding. If these qualities had caused Toole some pain in his life, they served him extraordinarily well after his death. According to Toole's biographer, René Pol Nevils, Thelma's 'narcissistic personality' was just what was needed to further her dead son's ambitions, by making them co-extensive with her own. 'She no longer had a son. He had failed her, and in turn, she was a failure. She thought that if she could get his book out there, get it published, then her son would be a success, and she would be a success.' In the end, they both were: yet another triumph for 'narcissism'.

Enter Walker Percy, then teaching at Loyola University, and the author of a string of well-received novels, of which *The Moviegoer* (1961) is the best known.

It is not entirely clear why Thelma Toole picked him, but she was unrelenting. She wrote to Percy, she rang him, she hounded him: her deceased son, she said, had 'written a great novel', an 'undiscovered masterpiece'. Percy *must* read it. Sometime in 1976, she actually showed up at Loyola, sat herself down in front of Percy's office, and demanded that he take the bulky, smeared, dog-eared carbon-copy manuscript, and *start reading*.

'Why would I want to do that?' said Percy firmly, remembering that 'over the years I have become very good at getting out of things I don't want to do'. But he had never had to deal with Thelma Toole before, and it was abundantly clear that he would waste less time reading than resisting. He took the manuscript, sent the pest away, and began to read. As he recalls in his Preface to the first edition:

> only one hope remained – that I could read a few pages and that they would be bad enough for me, in good conscience, to read no further. Usually I can do just that. Indeed the first paragraph often suffices. My only fear was that this one might not be bad enough, or might just be good enough, so that I would have to keep reading.

Sadly, at first, he read on, and further on, first bemused, then intrigued, and increasingly delighted:

surely it was not possible that it was so good. I shall resist the temptation to say what first made me gape, grin, laugh out loud, shake my head in wonderment . . . I hesitate to use the word comedy – though comedy it is – because that implies simply a funny book, and this novel is a great deal more than that. A great rumbling farce of Falstaffian dimensions would better describe it, commedia would come closer to it.

The search for a publisher began again, with Percy leading the hunt. But it was still four more years until, in 1980, Louisiana State University Press – an appropriate publisher but hardly a prestigious literary imprint – brought out the book. They did so out of admiration for the text, rather than any hope of profit, feeling, as Gottlieb had previously, that *Confederacy* was unlikely to sell.

The next year, *A Confederacy of Dunces* won the Pulitzer Prize for Fiction. Quickly hailed as *the* comic masterpiece of American literature, reviews were generally ecstatic, and astonished. Perhaps *Time Magazine*'s reviewer put it most simply, and best: 'If a book's price is measured against the laughs it provokes, *A Confederacy of Dunces* is the bargain of the year.'

It has, by now, been translated into eighteen languages, and sold over a million and a half copies. A biography of Toole has recently been published, a movie version of the novel is in production, Anthony Burgess chose it as one of his 99 best novels of the twentieth century. Copies of the first edition now fetch as much as £4,000 ($7,200) – many of them signed by Walker Percy, who, no doubt about it, had every right to do so. After all, there will be no copies signed by John Kennedy Toole.

Many years ago (when the first edition of *Confederacy* was still £200 ($360)) I bought, and quickly sold, Toole's paperback copy of *Finnegans Wake*, intelligently annotated by him in a finely formed, minuscule hand. It was riveting to trace Toole grappling with the master – perhaps for teaching purposes, maybe just for the fun of it. But on page 155, the annotation stopped, and the remaining pages were pristine. It was a fascinating symbolic object, which left me wondering what he would have made of the rest, before his engagement with it was so abruptly truncated. I wondered why he was unable, or unwilling, to go on?

I wish he had been able to use the services of my literary agent, the late, irrepressible Giles Gordon. An engaging speaker and controversialist, Giles was frequently invited to address literary societies. Fond of company, and kindly by nature, he often accepted these invitations, chewing chicken at the Lowestoft Literary Evening, or whatever and wherever. Rising to say his few words after dinner, he told me, he was inevitably confronted by a phalanx of anxious and earnest would-be novelists, of all sexes and persuasions. They listened to him politely, as he recalled, but they were really only there to ask their collective, single question: '*What* do I have to do to get my novel published.' The tone, as Giles (a good mimic) produced it, was querulous and aggrieved. Surely, it was inevitably put to him, publishing is a closed shop, run by the London literary Mafia for its own members, impossible to penetrate by an outsider, however talented? Equally surely he, one of the godfathers, could (if he wished) tell his interlocutors how to penetrate this closed circle. 'How *does* one get one's book published?'

Leaning forward from his place at the table or rostrum, Giles paused, sighed, and pushed his glasses down his nose, staring at the questioner as he did so.

'It's simple,' he said, with that cultivated acerbity that Edinburgh accents seem made for, 'write a good book!'

He might well have added: 'and if you do, have confidence in it. Keep your pecker up.' Alas, had John Kennedy Toole only done so. Surely, *Confederacy* would have found a publisher, and been followed by . . . what? A foolish enough question, like asking how Keats would have developed, but an irresistible one.

BRIDESHEAD REVISITED

They say that owners come to resemble their dogs. Or perhaps it is the other way round? I wouldn't know, never having owned a dog, not wishing to inflict my face on one. But a more unlikely proposition – that books come to resemble their authors – strikes me as having some validity.

Consider the following two novels, one published in 1928 and one in 1930. Both are clad in brightly coloured dustwrappers, with amusing, cartoon-like illustrations on the covers – witty, gay, childlike, insouciant. They are clearly intended to transmit something not only about their contents, but about their author: that becomes obvious when you realize that he designed them himself.

The first of these books is *Decline and Fall,* the second, *Vile Bodies.* Their author was Evelyn Waugh, and the very appearance of the books nominates him as a bright young thing of the late 1920s. And how different is this third book, published in 1944, severely bound in stiff blue-grey paper wrappers, with a simple label affixed, giving its title – *Brideshead Revisited* – and the name of the author, that self-same Evelyn Waugh.

The change from the brightness of tone and appearance of Waugh's early books to the sombre colour and typography of the *Brideshead* suggests, of course, something more than a change in the author's nature and self-presentation. *Brideshead* was published at the end of the Second World War and is, in part, a chronicle of the loss of innocence of a generation of young people who, having escaped the horrors of the trenches, had their relatively short and superficial period of gaiety brutally truncated by the events of the Second War.

Oddly, this unprepossessing volume was printed as a gift for Waugh's friends, and published in an edition of just 50 copies. It bears an inserted sticker, which announces, in the strictest tones:

This edition is privately printed for the author's friends; no copies are for sale. Messrs. Chapman and Hall earnestly request that until they announce the publication of the ordinary edition in the early part of 1945, copies will not be lent outside the circle for which they are intended, and no reference will appear to the book in the press.

I love the ambiguity of 'the circle for which they are intended', which strictly refers to those friends to whom Waugh sent the book, but which suggests persons of the right class.

It isn't clear, in the book trade, what this edition of *Brideshead* should be called. I have seen it referred to as a proof copy (which it is not, because proof copies are cheaply printed by publishers as an in-house trial run), nor is it a 'pre-publication' issue, though it precedes the first trade edition, which was published some six months later, with a revised text. What this is, quite simply, is the first edition of *Brideshead Revisited*, and it is, as you would imagine, very scarce.

Many copies of this edition of the book also bear a printed note apologizing for the fact that the author was unable to inscribe copies because of his war duties. In fact, though, most copies I have encountered were inscribed by Waugh to one friend or another. By far the most valuable of these was given to Graham Greene.

It was sometime in 1990 that I had a phone call from Greene, inquiring, in that slightly puckish tone that he liked to adopt, whether it was conceivable that I might be interested in his advance copy of *Brideshead*, 'with a little *dedicace* from Evelyn to me'?

'Distinctly,' I said, distinctly.

'Oh . . . good,' he replied, as if I had surprised him. (He was a lot of fun to deal with.)

'I could give you £6,000 ($11,000) for it,' I said. It was important to sound as if I knew what it was worth, but valuing a book of this sort is difficult, because it is unique. Other inscribed copies of the same issue had fetched less, but this one – being inscribed to Greene – was more desirable.

He didn't pause for thought. 'That will be fine. I'll have the book sent round to you.'

It is hard for me to price a book until I have it in my hands. It's a matter of acquaintance, of look, and feel. When the *Brideshead* arrived, in lovely condition, with its simple but perfect inscription ('For Graham Greene, this antiquated work, from Evelyn Waugh.'), I fell in love with it immediately and with every day that passed I loved it more and more, and it seemed to me more and more valuable. I had begun by thinking I might get £10,000 ($18,000) for it – a reasonable mark up – but as soon as I saw it, it went up to £12,000 ($22,000). Over the next few weeks I kept raising the price in my mind, as if the book (or my head) had a taxi meter attached to it, whirling round and round.

It soon sold for £16,000 ($29,000) to a member of the rare book trade. He didn't hesitate, leaving me with the unhappy impression that he might have paid more. This happens to me frequently. I call it Bertie's Paradox, after an observation made by my son when he was ten years old. I had reported to him, happily, that I had just sold a book for £12,500, and made a good profit. He thought for a moment.

'If it sold for that, I'll bet you could have got £13,000.'

'Probably,' I admitted.

'So why didn't you?'

'Look at it this way,' I said, in my best pedagogic mode, happy to teach him something. 'If I could have got £13,000, then surely I could have got £13,500?'

Bertie agreed.

'But then I could have got £14,000, right? And so on and so on. You could end up at a million.'

He saw what I meant, and nodded.

'I get it,' he said. 'But I still think you would have got £13,000! Five hundred pounds is a lot of money.'

Before cataloguing the *Brideshead* I rang Graham, to tell him of my revised estimate of its value, promising him a further, substantial, cheque when the book sold.

'Not at all,' he said. 'When we agree a price, that means I am happy with what I am getting. If you do well out of it, then good for you.'

So worldly, so generous, so wise. But he was also content because he had another copy of the book, the first trade edition (issued in 1945) with a similarly charming *dedicace*. I offered to buy that as well, but that was going too far.

'It's one of my favourite books,' he said, a little tartly, 'and I intend to reread it.' I toyed with the idea of sending him a Penguin copy to reread, but decided against it.

Brideshead Revisited was begun in 1943, but Waugh

was unable to get a sustained run at the manuscript, working on it between various missions and tours of duty, particularly in Yugoslavia and Italy. He had a relatively peaceful war, much of it swanning about with various pals in foreign parts, trying to find congenial company and decent food. Irascible at the best of times, he was not exactly a model soldier. One of his postings ended within twenty-four hours, when he was rebuked by his commanding officer after imbibing too much drink over dinner, and Waugh responded airily that he did not see why he 'should change the habits of a lifetime for a whim of his'. The problem was compounded by the fact that Waugh had already spilled a glass of claret into the officer's lap.

It is no wonder, then, that when Waugh applied to the War Office for indefinite leave to work on his novel, his superiors were astonished, reflected for just a moment, and agreed. Waugh had made his case persuasively. He was a rotten soldier. He was, he pointed out, too old, technically incompetent, physically inert, administratively inexperienced, linguistically limited, and preoccupied with the need for literary composition. Since it was 'understood that entertainment is now regarded as a legitimate contribution to the war effort', surely, Waugh maintained, it would be preferable to have him writing well than soldiering badly. And anyway, he pointed out, it was difficult to support his large family on a lieutenant's pay.

It is hard to imagine such an argument working today, but I rather suspect that the Army was as keen to have a rest from Waugh as he was from it. Leave was granted, and he was soon off at a hotel in Devon – his usual mode when writing – working on a novel called *The Household of the Faith*. It was to become *Brideshead Revisited*. The work was something of a new departure for him, the prose pitched at a higher rhetorical level than in his previous novels, a new level of seriousness attained. Always methodical and disciplined, he knew to the word how much he had written on any day, or week. For the first time, however, Waugh began to revise while still in the process of composition, and it pained him how slow the process was: 'I have fallen into a slough of rewriting. Every day I seem to go over what I did the day before and make it shorter. I am getting spinsterish about style.'

He moved to the Hyde Park Hotel after Easter, nominally working as a journalist so as to prolong his leave. He made steady progress with his 'Magnum Opus', which was getting so long, he reported to his literary agent A.D. Peters, that it was 'turning into a Jeroboam'. Though eventually recalled to the Army, work on the novel progressed steadily, and he finished it in June of 1944.

He was uncharacteristically pleased with the result: *Brideshead* was, he believed, his masterpiece, a sombre eschatalogical work, filled with 'hope, not indeed, that anything but disaster lies ahead, but that the human spirit, redeemed, can survive all disasters'. Once finished, the book was quickly typeset, bound at Waugh's expense, and the limited edition sent as a Christmas present to his family and close friends.

If Waugh had intended *Brideshead* as a proverbial gift horse, it was the job of his friends to look it in the mouth. Like most writers, he solicited criticism, and was unduly sensitive when it came. He was most grateful for corrections with regard to matters of fact, as when Father Ronald Knox assisted with details about the consecration of chapels. Nancy Mitford (who had the good sense, first, to proclaim the book 'a classic') helped him on a question of fashion: 'one dreadful error. Diamond clips were only invented about 1930, you wore a diamond *arrow* in your cloche.'

He was more anxious about responses to the book's (relatively modest) sexual explicitness. The passages concerning Julia's adultery with Charles had given him great difficulty:

> I feel very much the futility of describing sexual emotions without describing the sexual act; I should like to give as much detail as I have of the meals, to the two coitions . . . It would be no more or less obscene to leave them to the reader's imagination, which in this case cannot be as acute as mine.

I rather doubt it: the word 'coitions' gives the game away. When we refer to one of the relevant passages, the problem becomes obvious. When Ryder first makes love to Julia, Waugh's description carries all of the author's unease and embarrassment:

> I took formal possession of her as a lover . . . Now on the rough water, as I made free of her narrow loins . . . while the waves still broke and thundered on the prow, the act of possession was a symbol, a rite of ancient origin and solemn meaning.

Not much fun for a girl in that, it's no wonder the affair fizzled out. The passage, as Graham Greene remarked, is hapless. It was entirely rewritten, and improved a little, for the revised edition which was published in 1960. But Waugh was no more comfortable describing 'coition', than, one supposes, he was doing it.

Katherine Asquith could hardly bring herself to read her advance copy of *Brideshead*, and Waugh's wife Laura was a little embarrassed by the relevant passages, and had the wit not to say so. His clerical friends were surprisingly supportive. If Waugh had to describe the sexual act, at least it was regarded and described as a sacrament.

Whatever his reservations about the final text, Waugh was pleased with the result, and relieved to be finished. 'I have never been happier,' he wrote to Laura, 'I see nothing but innocent pleasure ahead.' He was certain that the work was a masterpiece, and the public agreed. The book sold out immediately, though it was not reprinted because of paper shortages.

His financial future was ensured when the book, after first publication, was purchased by the American Book of the Month Club, and sold three quarters of a million copies. He was offered $150,000 (£83,000) for the film rights, but eventually declined when he couldn't ensure adequate control of the script.

To celebrate, Waugh commissioned a bust of himself by a sculptor named Paravicini, which I am sorry never to have seen. Waugh's biographer describes it as 'suggesting the priggish benignity of an Anglican headmaster bishop'. (*Both* a bishop and a headmaster?) Waugh confessed to Laura that he rather liked it:

It is very masterly & rather bad tempered in expression but most forceful like Beethoven rather. It will be a lovely possession for you & indeed a series of possessions for all as I propose to have it cast in bronze and terra cotta & lead and to travel with it as Gerald Wellesley used to travel with the bust of his great ancestor. You can imagine what an interest and excitement it has been to me.

This would be intolerable were it not subtly self-mocking. When he eventually took possession of one of the busts, Waugh put it on his sideboard, with a cap on it at a rakish angle. He always had a taste for the grotesque and absurd, and liked making himself the object of his own ridicule.

Riches didn't entirely suit Waugh: he could indulge his taste for buying grand houses, collecting Victoriana, building his library, and adding to his wine cellar. But he missed the anxiety of having to write for money, which honed his mind, and sharpened his appetites. In latter years, his temper sharpened, his snobbery increased, his misanthropy deepened. You can see the change from the very appearance of his postwar books. None of his later books, when you look at their covers, suggest the gaiety of spirit of his early work. None, indeed, has even the solemn austerity that is conveyed by the stiff blue-grey covers of the first edition of *Brideshead Revisited*.

THE TALE OF
PETER RABBIT

I suspect that, in my innocence, I trusted him because he was a doctor. Doctors, to a kid, have an immeasurable, calm authority. They might prod you painfully, or stick needles in you, but it was for your own good. But this doctor was different, this doctor was fun. Imagine how much less exciting it would have been had he been called *Mr* Seuss. Seuss? Even that was enticing, because it sounded like a creature in one of his own books. *The Seuss Meets a Moose*, something like that.

In fact, he was as fictional as a Grinch. He was neither a doctor, nor was he called Seuss. Theodor (Seuss) Geisel, the grandson of German immigrants, was born in Springfield, Massachusetts in 1904. A graduate of Dartmouth, who later attended Oxford, he won three Academy Awards before publishing his first book in 1937. The pseudonym 'Dr Seuss' was presumably intended to have just the effect it produced on me. I believed in him entirely. He was the real thing.

I adored the strange and brightly coloured drawings of his creatures, and was thrilled by their outlandish behaviour: the anarchic frenzy of *The Cat in the Hat*, the unseemly grandiosity of *Yertle the Turtle*. For my generation of children, Dr Seuss was not so much a favourite author, as the only author, and we derived a pretty considerable sense of our world from his books. It was, in most respects, a grey, conformist time, yet here was this maelstrom of whirling energy and infinite possibility, improbably peopled, yet reassuringly able to right itself just before disaster struck. It was profoundly cheerful and optimistic, quintessentially American.

The equivalently loved English children's author is, of course, Beatrix Potter, who had every bit as profound an influence on several generations of English children as my beloved Dr Seuss did on American ones. I rather doubt whether Potter's influence remains as strong as it was – she died, after all, in 1943, and the first of her books, *The Tale of Peter Rabbit*, was first published in 1901. Today's children are more interested in *Harry* Potter.

The gentle pastoral qualities of Beatrix's world, inhabited by animals who are fuzzy toys incarnate, safe and dependable, gives us some retrospective insight into an England now virtually extinct: rural, familiar, whimsical, cosy. Though Peter is assiduously hunted by Farmer McGregor, he is never caught, for Potter's natural world is not red, but pink, in tooth and claw. Like William Wordsworth, she was a Londoner, and her 'nature' is idealized, sanitized, more concept than reality. Both writers had a profound effect on the English psyche. England is virtually the only place in the world in which it is regarded as both bracing and morally improving to go for a walk in the country. In most countries, when you do that you'll get bitten by the small animals, or eaten by the large ones.

For three generations there can hardly have been a child's bedroom throughout middle England, that didn't have a little shelf full of well-thumbed Beatrix Potters, their covers dusty and marked, with (more often than not) the scrawls and doodles of some childish admirer throughout the text.

That's the problem with children's books. Children handle them, with grubby little hands. They love the rhythm and repetition of the same story, read over and over until they know it by heart. Rereading is one of the delights of childhood. It makes the world safe and predictable, but it's murder on the books.

So when it comes to collecting children's books, which is a form of nostalgia engaged in largely by the middle-aged, intent on recapturing some of the magic of childhood, it is nearly impossible to find the books in the right condition. You know what Beatrix Potters look like: there are rows of them for sale in any book-shop, and the format is much the same as it was from the start. They look terrific, the small illustrated covers crisp and unstained, the pages in pristine order. They should look like that, they're new.

But when you find a first edition Beatrix Potter, now some hundred or so years old, in pristine condition, you have a sense of something gone wrong. Why doesn't it look used? Was the book bought as a present, put away, and never given? Why not? Did the present-giver decide against giving the book? Might the child have died? Or was the book given into a family so obsessed by orderliness that it had to be treated as a hallowed object, rather than as the functional amuse-ment that Beatrix Potter intended? Whatever the reason, one thing is certain: if you can find one of the first few Beatrix Potter first editions, in fine condition, it will be worth a lot of money, and avidly sought after. The collectors of children's books are more than usually obsessional.

Beatrix Potter's life, almost comically, can be described as moving from one Victorian stereotype to another, to another. Born in 1866, she began as a lonely child taking refuge in fantasy, became a lonely spinster sublimating her unhappiness through her work, and ended making a late happy marriage, after which she gave up authorship entirely.

From the earliest time she could remember, Beatrix

Potter had her head crammed full of stories and pictures. Brought up in comfortable circumstances in London, though by stern and remote parents, she was deprived of formal education. Left to her own devices, she drew and studied assiduously, and took twelve oil painting classes at the age of seventeen. As she observed in her journal: 'It is all the same, drawing, painting, modelling, the irresistible desire to copy any beautiful object which strikes the eye. Why cannot one be content to look at it? I must draw, however poor the result.'

She went round the galleries and museums compulsively, and her earliest influences showed discrimination: she adored Turner, Richard Doyle and Gustave Doré, and admired the 'somewhat niggling but absolutely genuine admiration for copying natural details' of the Pre-Raphaelites. The painter Millais, a family friend, admired her early work, observing, 'plenty of people can draw, but you . . . have observation.'

In 1890 she designed six greeting cards, and sent them to Hildesheimer & Faulkner, the German publishers. To her surprise, they were pleased with the work, paid her £6 ($11), and asked to see more. Three years later she produced a series of pictures of rabbits and other animals for a book called *A Happy Pair*, published by the same firm.

Yet she had no intention of becoming anything so

grand as a writer or painter. Much of her earliest work consists of illustrated letters written to the children of friends, on their birthdays, at Christmas, or when they were ill. At the time, the writing of illustrated letters was still commonplace: Lewis Carroll did them, and Edward Lear, and, later, John Betjeman. They were written to amuse both the recipient and the writer.

Peter Rabbit first appears in one of these letters in September of 1893 (when Beatrix Potter was twenty-seven), written to Noel Moore, the five-year-old son of her former German teacher and companion, Annie Carter. The story is instantly recognizable:

> I don't know what to write you, so I shall tell you a story about four little rabbits, whose names were Flopsy, Mopsy, Cottontail and Peter. They lived with their mother in a sand bank under the root of a big fir tree.

Accompanying the story are pictures of the four rabbits, with the insouciant Peter given pride of place. Even in this early incarnation, the story bears all the hallmarks of Beatrix Potter's mature style, which seems so simple as to be effortless. It is not.

> My usual method of writing is to scribble, and cut out, and write it again and again. The shorter and plainer the better . . . I think the great point in

writing for children is to have something to say and to say it in simple direct language . . . I polish! Polish! Polish! To the last revise.

Her childish readers – and their parents – greatly admired her picture letters, saved them assiduously, showed them to their friends, and begged for more. It was enough to make a girl think of publication. Seven years later, Miss Potter wrote to inquire, perhaps a trifle disingenuously, whether Noel happened to have kept that letter about that rabbit? And if so, might she borrow it?

He had, and she could. She soon rewrote the story, and produced a further set of pen-and-ink illustrations. Adding a coloured frontispiece, showing the ill Peter being given camomile tea by his mother, she wrapped the story in card wrappers, and entitled it *The Tale of Peter Rabbit and Mr McGregor's Garden*, by H.B. Potter. During the years 1900 and 1901, the story was sent to six publishers, none of whom showed much interest, partly, it seems, because the book was thought too small and too short to be of commercial interest. But Potter stuck to her guns saying she 'would rather make two or three little books costing 1/- each, than one big book costing 6/- because she thinks little rabbits cannot afford to spend six shillings on one book'.

Her solution was to publish the book herself. She had line-blocks made for the black-and-white drawings, and a three-coloured frontispiece was produced, for an edition of 250 copies. On 16 December – just in time for Christmas – the books arrived, covered in grey-green paper covers, with a picture of four rabbits on them, entitled *The Tale of Peter Rabbit*. They made perfect Christmas gifts for her many friends, and the rest she sold off at a half-penny apiece. Arthur Conan Doyle was amongst her first admirers, and bought a copy for his children.

The books were gone within a couple of weeks, and in February a second edition of some 200 copies was issued, in a slightly better binding, olive-green covers, and with a few minor textual changes. These copies bear the date 'February 1902', whereas the first 250 were undated.

But just before the first of these privately printed editions came out, the London publishing firm of Frederick Warne decided that it would, after all, like to publish what it called her 'quaint little Bunny Book'. The only stipulation they made, fortunately, was that all of the illustrations should be in colour.

Miss Potter set to work immediately, but was full of self-doubt:

> I wish the drawings had been better; I dare say they may look better when reduced; but I am becoming so tired of them, I begin to think they are positively bad . . . My brother is sarcastic about the figures;

what you and he take for Mr McGregor's nose, was intended for his ear, not his nose at all.

These original drawings for *Peter Rabbit* survive today in the archive of Frederick Warne. They have been kept in pristine condition all these years, carefully preserved in tissue in a drawer. When examined, they have all the freshness of the day they were painted, for water-colour, sadly, fades when exposed to sunlight. Though unlikely to come on the market, I imagine that they would be worth at least £100,000 ($180,000). Each.

Though both writer and publisher were uncertain about the book's prospects, *Peter Rabbit* was an immediate success. Eight thousand copies were issued in October of 1902, followed by a further 12,000 the next month, and another 8,000 the next. Warne reprinted and reprinted, and the public bought and bought. Peter Rabbit had become, almost overnight, one of the most greatly loved characters of children's fiction. Soon after publication, the book was given the ultimate accolade, and was pirated in America. At thirty-six, Beatrix Potter had come of age.

Sadly, Peter – one of Beatrix Potter's favourite pets – never lived to celebrate his new fame. In one of her privately printed copies, Miss Potter wrote the following obituary notice:

In affectionate remembrance of poor old Peter Rabbit, who died on the 26th of January, 1901 at the end of his 9th year. He was bought, at a very tender age, in the Uxbridge Road, Shepherds Bush, for the exorbitant sum of 4/6 - . . . whatever the limitations of his intellect or outward shortcomings of his fur, and his ears and toes, his disposition was uniformly amiable and his temper unfailingly sweet. An affectionate companion and a quiet friend.

As he has been to his many admirers, especially to those lucky enough to own a first edition of the charming book based on his exploits.

Over the next thirteen years, Miss Potter produced twenty more books, refusing to compromise her unrelentingly high standards. She sometimes had cause to argue with Warne about the production values of the books. Like most great children's writers – like most great writers – she kept up her standards because her most critical and crucial audience was herself:

If it were not impertinent to lecture one's publisher – you are a great deal too afraid of the public, for whom I have never cared one tupenny button. I am sure that it is that attitude of mind which has enabled me to keep up the series. Most people, after one success, are so cringingly afraid of doing less well that they rub all the edge off their subsequent work.

Beatrix Potter had a close relationship, of which her parents greatly disapproved, with her publisher Norman Warne, to whom she became engaged in 1905. Tragically, he died of leukaemia less than a month later. But in October of 1913, Potter married William Heelis, a solicitor whom she had met some four years previously, when purchasing a farm with the earnings from her work. It was the happiest and most fulfilling period of her life. As she had previously confessed to her diary:

> Latter-day fate ordains that many women shall be unmarried and self-contained, nor should I personally dream to complain, but I hold an old-fashioned notion that a happy marriage is the crown of a woman's life.

It was a happy marriage, and Mrs Heelis never again published a book in England, though she did oversee the vast industry of Potter artefacts: stuffed animals, ornaments, dolls, toys, mugs, and knick-knacks, while pursuing the life of a countrywoman and sheep farmer.

What a waste, you might think, but it has always seemed to me the right end to her story. She had done her best work, and profited from it considerably. She had worked alone, bravely and to the highest standard, and there was little left for her but to repeat past efforts. Though she insisted on keeping up her standards, her later books feel a little tired. Enough to say that she has delighted generations of children, and tens of millions of readers in virtually every language, including Braille. Collectors have profited from her as well. A nice copy of one of the first 250 privately printed *Peter Rabbits* would now set you back £40,000 ($72,000), and even the first Frederick Warne copies are worth a couple of thousand. (By way of contrast, my old pal *The Cat in the Hat* is only worth about £4,000 ($7,200) in first edition.)

These prices are for copies in excellent condition, of course, with the nice final irony that the books so treasured by today's collectors must have been unloved by the children who first owned them. They wouldn't look so perfect if they had been properly loved.

THREE STORIES AND
TEN POEMS

My aunt Millicent is retired now, but she used to prac-
tise as a psychoanalyst. She once told me, with great
satisfaction, about her patient, Bernie the dentist, who,
after years on the couch, confessed to her that he no
longer felt hostile to his patients. He had, he noted,
recently told his Wednesday golfing partners – also
dentists – about his inner transformation. They were
astonished: it is impossible, they avowed, for a dentist
not to feel hostile to his patients.

You may already have postulated some purpose in
this – if, for dentists, you read rare book dealers, and
for patients, customers, you may locate a correlative
psychological syndrome. I'm sorry to admit that I suffer
from the problem myself. Not with regard to all book
collectors, but certainly towards a significant minority.
These are, by and large, American, rich, and highly
acquisitive. This is a loveable combination of attributes.
But the problem is that they all are in search of the

same rare books, and they want them to look as if they were new.

Price differentials between normally used copies of first editions, and unblemished ones have always been considerable, but they've now become absurd. At a recent sale in New York, a copy of Ernest Hemingway's first book, *Three Stories and Ten Poems*, which was published in Paris in 1923, appeared in such superb condition that it could have been mistaken for new. Though only 300 copies were printed, it is not all that rare, and if you've got the money you can usually find one. Only a few months previously, a pretty example sold for £22,000 ($40,000) in London. The one in New York made some £70,000 ($126,000). Why? You'll hardly believe it, but it was because it had its original glassine wrapper. Not a printed dustwrapper, mind you – it never had one – just an outer covering of the stationer's glassine (a kind of brittle, translucent tissue, beloved of the French) in which it had been issued.

Though that glassine sleeve is rare, *Three Stories and Ten Poems* is unusually common in fine condition. I am told that, sometime in the late 1960s, an imaginative American book scout visited Darantiere's printing works in Dijon to inquire if they cared to sell 'any more stock'. He was met by a series of Gallic shrugs, when someone remembered that, yes, there were some old books on the shelves of the storeroom. The runner bought them all. Included was a box full of mint copies of *Three Stories and Ten Poems*, for which he was charged the original price of two dollars.

In appearance, *Three Stories and Ten Poems* is a perfect example of the slim, privately printed books of the period, with its home-made charm, attractive typographical grey covers, and surprisingly good quality printing. It hasn't the blandness and uniformity of many of the regularly published books of the time.

He may have been the new kid in town but people had heard of Ernest Hemingway. He'd arrived in Paris, two years earlier, with his new wife Hadley, and letters of introduction to Ezra Pound, Gertrude Stein and Sylvia Beach. He was a muscular, bouncy journalist – the literary incarnation of Pooh's friend Tigger – who had published a few prose pieces and poems. Stein found him attractive, and was delighted by how 'passionately interested' he was in ideas, especially hers. Pound soon declared him 'the finest prose stylist in the world'.

In a literary era dominated by the opulent prose of Virginia Woolf and D.H. Lawrence, or the obscure modernism of Gertrude Stein and Joyce, the ascetic voice of Hemingway seemed to have a pared-down perfection. In the words of his biographer Carlos Baker, his style was 'precise and exact, yet highly connotative, sparse and bare, yet charged with poetic intensity'.

Take, for instance, the opening sentences of the short story 'Up in Michigan', from *Three Stories and Ten Poems*.

Jim Gilmore came from Hortons Bay in Canada. He bought the Blacksmith shop from old man Horton. Jim was short and dark with big moustaches and big hands.

Admirers loved the suggestiveness of the writing, the little that it included and the large terrain that it managed both to withhold and to suggest. Here are the archetypal rhythms of the American mid-West, the voice of a plain-speaking but sensitive man, distrustful of ornament, excess, almost of language itself. It is striking, to be sure, but I often wonder if Hemingway wasn't simply an adept who found the right prose style both to enact, and to conceal, the limited range of his vision, and the crimped range of his sympathies.

But who am I to say? Everyone loved him. Visiting Pound in Italy, Hemingway was lucky enough to be introduced to Robert McAlmon and Edward O'Brien, who were to be instrumental in shaping his early career. McAlmon, an American expat and writer, with a rich English wife, immediately offered to publish Hemingway's first book at his Contact Publishing Company, which he had founded largely, one suspects, to ensure an outlet for his own work. O'Brien, the editor of a series of books that anthologized the best American short stories published each year, immediately accepted a story of Hemingway's. He was so impressed by his new find, in fact, that he asked

Hemingway if he might dedicate the 1923 volume to him. Hemingway was thrilled to bits: 'I will make a very solemn vow to you and God never to think about any readers but you and God when writing stories all the rest of my life . . .'

One of the best books in my own tiny collection of first editions is a copy of *Three Stories and Ten Poems*, bearing an inscription to Edward J. O'Brien from Hemingway. Significantly enough, this is written below the printed dedication of the book: 'This book is for Hadley', under which Hemingway adds, 'and this one is for Edward J. O'Brien from Ernest Hemingway'. Which leads one to the conclusion that, so strongly did Hemingway feel about O'Brien's beneficent intervention in his career, that he created a second dedicatee for the book. (I like to think that this makes the book more valuable than that crazy one at auction, but I have my doubts.)

The Best Short Stories of 1923, when it came out in January of 1924, contained Hemingway's story 'My Old Man'. And, as O'Brien had promised, he gave Hemingway the singular honour of the volume's dedication. The only problem was that the dedication read 'To Ernest Hemenway'. Given that this was Hemingway's first published book appearance in America, and first in any anthology, this appalling howler, which was repeated in several other places in the book, was unforgivable. Hemingway recalled the episode, many years later in *A Moveable Feast*, observing proudly that O'Brien had broken his own rules in printing a story that had not appeared previously, and noting the misspelling of his name. But Hemingway was a practical fellow, and disliked holding a grudge. Within a couple of years, he had got over his irritation, and used a quote from O'Brien on the dustwrapper of the first American edition of *In Our Time* in 1926.

The 300 copies of *Three Stories and Ten Poems* that McAlmon produced in July of 1923 cost $2.00 each, and even in its tiny format (just 7 x 4 1/2 inches) the text only ran to fifty-five pages. Six of the poems had been published previously in *Poetry* Magazine, but the short stories were new (and *very* short). No-one could have argued that the poems were particularly good (or had much to do with the stories), though Hemingway was keen on them. They were really there, like the excessive number of blank pages at the start and finish, to bulk up the book. Because three stories and ten poems were, in fact, all that Hemingway had. It was his entire literary output, because his wife Hadley had lost the rest.

The story has been told many times, has been the subject of plays and novels, and has many versions. But the facts are clear. Deciding to join Hemingway in Lausanne (where he was covering the Peace Conference) in November of 1922, Hadley packed her bag, and headed for the Gare de Lyon. Lovingly, she brought along Ernest's manuscripts in case he wanted to work on them: hand-written material, typescripts, and (foolishly) carbon copies of all of his work. Included was the draft of a novel, eleven short stories, and a quantity of poems.

At the railway station, thirsty and alone, she walked off in search of an Evian and an English newspaper, asking a porter (according to the most sympathetic accounts) to keep an eye on her suitcase. When she returned, a few moments later, it was gone. When she eventually met Hemingway in Lausanne, she was so distraught that he found it impossible to discover what the matter was. Was she having an affair? Had she fallen in love with someone else? Worse, she indicated tearfully. And then (according to one of Hemingway's friends) he blurted out his most potent fear: 'Then you've slept with a Negro, tell me!'

It was a lot worse than that, she blubbed: his manuscripts were gone, all of them. Utterly distraught, Hemingway took the next train back to Paris, and searched the Gare de Lyon from top to bottom. Nothing. His life's work (except for two short stories, one at the bottom of a drawer, the other sent out to a publisher) was gone. He realized immediately that the lost material was unduplicatable, because it had 'the lyric facility of boyhood that was as perishable and deceptive as youth was'. According to Hadley, 'I think he never recovered from the pain of this irreparable loss.' For a time, he felt he would never write again, but was eventually reassured by the tough advice of Gertrude Stein: start again, 'concentrate!' Perhaps it was a blessing in disguise. She hadn't much admired the early work anyway and, in retrospect, neither did Hemingway. As he later observed in *A Moveable Feast*, 'it was probably good for me.'

Adding 'Out of Season' to the surviving two stories, with the ballast of the ten poems and lots of blank leaves, Hemingway soon cobbled together his first book. It was enthusiastically promoted by Pound and McAlmon, printed in Dijon by Darantiere, and distributed through Sylvia Beach's Shakespeare and Company: 'the same gang,' Hemingway announced proudly, 'that published *Ulysses*.'

Unlike *Ulysses*, which had been widely reviewed when it came out in the previous year, scarcely anybody noticed *Three Stories and Ten Poems*, with the exception of Hemingway's mother, Grace. Since he had been a teenager, she had found his writing morbid, and she was particularly shocked by her son's use of the real names of family friends for the randy lovers in 'Up in Michigan'. Within a couple of years, she had banned his writing from her house and announced that 'every page fills me with sick loathing.' She particularly hated *The Sun Also Rises*, damning it as 'one of the filthiest books of the year', a judgement that has a suspicious knowingness about it.

Saddened by the absence of any considered response, Hemingway sent a copy of the book to the American critic Edmund Wilson, who rather liked it, and mentioned it briefly some time later in *The Dial*. But the relative lack of attention didn't matter: *In Our Time* was published in Paris in 1924, and in America the following year, and Hemingway was on his way. Within a few years he was complaining that even he didn't own a copy of *Three Stories and Ten Poems*, and that he certainly wasn't going to pay the going rate of $150 for one – it 'would be like the snake eating his own tail to pay'. The first copy to appear at auction fetched $130 in 1932. Since that time, the book has appeared regularly in the sale rooms, sometimes accompanied by that flimsy and elusive glassine dust jacket, which the market has decided is worth some £50,000 ($90,000) of extra value. There is apparently nothing more alluring than this: a pristine copy, eighty years old, unravaged by time.

All I ask, in the gleaming light of such perfection, is: Why? With antique furniture we value the effects of time on the surface of an object, and call it patina; with paintings, we howl when inept restorers reproduce the way an oil painting would have looked on the day it was painted. The criterion that an object be in perfect, original condition is usually reserved for the collecting of piffling doo-dahs – of stamps, teddy bears, or dinky toys. But books? Books?

How did this happen? And for what reason? What, as an analyst might inquire, is the pathology behind it? Because this ludicrous insistence on perfect condition strikes one more as a symptom than a rational goal.

I'm a mere amateur at such things, but even I can tell when something screwy is going on. Anyway, it upsets me, and makes me tetchier. My friends suggested I seek the counsel of Aunt Milly.

She listened with the characteristic care of the therapist. 'There are several things conjoined here,' she said thoughtfully. 'First, I suppose, is the possession of the virgin. The collector gets some special, erotic pleasure from the unsullied quality of the object, which is his alone to fondle. It puts him – I presume we are talking about men here, aren't we? – in an intimate relation to the object.'

This seemed to me good sense.

'And yet,' she added, 'as is often true with forms of displaced sexual activity, there is a great deal of fear here as well . . .'

'Fear?' I asked.

'Of contagion, of being caught in some illicit activity, of which one is ashamed . . .'

'Come on, Auntie,' I said hastily, 'we're talking book collecting here . . .'

'The book is encased in a perfect wrapper, and then both are enclosed in a box. Prophylaxis is certainly involved. A morbid fear of contagion can be inferred, I think . . .'

'Contagion?'

'Well, sweetie,' she said (she is a very affectionate aunt), 'we live in a world in which the fear of Aids is almost as acute as the fear of ageing. Almost everyone is terrified of death, fearful about sex, and wants to look and remain young forever.'

'Do you mean . . .' I began, in astonishment.

'Exactly!' she said. 'They seek some surrogate activity. The book becomes the objective correlative of the state of being they yearn for, as well as a talisman warding off all that they most fear. That's why your little Hemingway book was so expensive.'

'So?' I asked thoughtfully, hardly able to take this all in.

'So,' she said firmly, 'from a psychoanalytic point of view, book collecting is a very rational activity indeed, and you shouldn't let it upset you.'

'Thanks, Auntie,' I said. 'You've helped me a lot. Wait 'til I tell my friends!'

'Maybe I should introduce you to Bernie,' she said. 'You like golf, don't you? You should get out more.'

AFTER TWO YEARS

One of the favourite games of rare book dealers is a variant of the 'I bet you didn't know that . . .' form of one-upmanship beloved of pedants of all persuasions. What we particularly enjoy is when we know something that a standard book of reference either gets wrong or, better yet, omits entirely. You will feel a 'for instance' coming: the magisterial *Cambridge Bibliography of English Literature* is universally recognized as the most reliable record of the publication histories of hundreds of English authors. Even that august publication, I am happy to tell you, fails to mention a book of Graham Greene's, published in 1949, entitled *After Two Years*. But I know all about it, and would be delighted to fill you in on the details.

In the autumn of 1989, I was frequently in Antibes, visiting my new friend Graham Greene, manically acquiring from him a spectacular range of manuscript material, including his travel and dream diaries, and letters to his mistress, Yvonne Cloetta. It was heady stuff, and I was just about to conclude that things could hardly get better than this, when they did. One evening, as we were driving off for dinner at La Colombe d'Or in St-Paul-de-Vence, between anxious pleas for me to slow down, Graham said, 'If you could be bothered to pick them up, I no longer need my copies of my own books.' I slowed down.

'*All* of your own copies?' I asked.

'All of them. But I'm afraid they're in my Paris flat. If you think it's worth it, I could have someone meet you there.' His expression didn't seem to change as he gazed nervously at the oncoming traffic, but I could hear the smile in his voice. He had spent sufficient personal time chasing books for his own collections to understand what it was that he was offering.

It is a sign of something unimaginative in me that all I could think of, in the first instance, was dust-wrappers. *Brighton Rock* is distinctly scarce in the wrapper, and even then was worth £5,000 ($9,000) – and I have recently seen one for ten times that. *Rumour at Nightfall* is even scarcer, though somewhat less valuable. Surely Greene would have kept pristine copies of his own books? I should have known better. I was, by then, tolerably familiar with his Antibes library, and had seen his collection of Victorian detective fiction. He had an eye for rarity, and was sensitive to bibliographic variation, but he had never been a fetishist about condition. If this was true of his own collections, it would surely apply to his own books?

A couple of weeks later, accompanied by his French literary agent, I stood in the bedroom of Greene's flat on the Boulevard Malesherbes, gazing into a closet that had been amateurishly shelved to contain, not Greene's underpants, but Greene's Greenes. It was immediately clear – rare books dealers can spot a rarity on a set of shelves at a single glance – that I was initially going to be disappointed. No dustwrappers on the two key books. Like most Greene collectors, he had the easy ones in wrappers *(The Man Within, Stamboul Train, It's a Battlefield)* and lacked most of the hard ones.

The disappointment lasted only a moment, like that of a father who wants a boy, only to discover immediately that his new-born girl is the best possible sort of new human. For tucked away in a corner were not one, but two copies of each of Greene's rarest books: *After Two Years* (1949) and *For Christmas* (1951), which even R.A. Wobbe, Greene's bibliographer, had failed to note. I had heard of them, vaguely, though I don't remember how, or when. Printed in editions of 25 and 12 copies by the Rosaio Press, these little books of poetry were not sufficiently known even to have become legendary rarities. Nobody seemed to know anything about them.

The Rosaio Press published only these two books. It took its name from the Anacapri villa Greene bought in 1948 for £3,000 ($5,400) (the income from his film work on *The Third Man*), and which he inhabited from time to time with his lover, Catherine Walston. An American beauty married to the Labour peer Lord (Harry) Walston, Catherine was later to serve as the model for Sarah, the heroine in *The End of the Affair*, which is dedicated to her (as 'C').

The copies in Greene's bedroom closet were Number 1 of each book (Greene's own copies, with additional poems written on the rear end papers), and Number 2 (Catherine Walston's copies, bearing long and loving inscriptions by her to Greene). Though the simple printed white wrappers were sufficiently discreet, the contents were deeply affectionate (a favourite word of Greene's), if poetically unimpressive. I will refrain from quoting any of the poems, out of deference to my old friend, and my reader's aesthetic sensibilities. Suffice it to say that the poems were sincere, loving, prosaic, and private. Rather sweet, really. You can get the flavour of them from a poem written at the same period, and on the same subject, which Greene later published in *A Quick Look Behind*, in 1983.

> I can believe only in love that strikes suddenly
> out of a clear sky;
> I do not believe in the slow germination of friend-
> ship
> Or one that asks 'why?'

Because our love came savagely, suddenly,
like an act of war,
I cannot conceive a love that rises gently
and subsides without a scar.

Certainly, there were to be scars aplenty – and not
merely of the sort that Greene occasionally produced
upon himself with cigarettes. At the onset of the affair,
sometime early in 1947, Greene had two young children with his wife Vivien in Oxford, and a long-term
mistress, Dorothy Glover, in London. With the coming
of Catherine (who had five young children of her own)
Greene's life became increasingly unstable. Glover
fought and fought, and eventually gave him up. In
November, Greene left Vivien.

In the light of these manifold conflicts of emotional
interest, it would have been foolish, and unkind, to
have distributed even small quantities of poems in
praise of his new mistress. Greene was later to tell me
that 'I don't think we ever sent out any copies.' Greene
and Catherine gave copies to each other, and copy
Number 3 of *After Two Years* was sent to Bontie Duran,
Catherine's older sister, and the couple's major confi-
dante during their affair. The inscription read: 'For
Bontie with great love from the two of us. Graham',
and the book was sold at Sotheby's in February 2000,
for £18,000 ($32,500), which was, remarkably, a good
deal less than a nice, dustwrapped *Brighton Rock*

would have cost you at that time. But the rare book market has become fixated on what are called 'big books' – the obvious rarities, preferably in superlative condition – and few collectors these days have the sophistication to pay a very large price for an obscure little volume like *After Two Years*.

Not merely an obscure little volume but an excessively rare one, the scarcest in the Greene canon. I felt a little greedy, carting away both sets of the books. Reluctantly, I asked Greene if he didn't wish to keep a set?

He thought for a moment.

'No. I don't need them now.'

I quickly packed them away with the other books destined to go back to England with me that evening, anxious that continued sight of them might make him change his mind. I need not have worried. Once he had agreed to a deal or course of action, he never deviated from it. In any case, it was many years since he had parted from Catherine, and the final love of his life, Yvonne Cloetta, was sitting beside him as we spoke. She seemed quietly pleased by his decision.

She was less pleased by Greene's suggestion that I purchase the letters that he had written to her over the many years of their relationship. Could such a sale be entirely discreet, she asked anxiously. No, I replied, you can never be certain – you can sell such material to the world's most discreet person, then he gets run over by a bus, and his widow puts the material into Sotheby's . . .

'Never mind that,' said Graham, 'it'll be fine.' Yvonne acceded uneasily, and I wrote her a substantial cheque, which seemed markedly to improve her mood. But when, some years later, the letters were quietly resold, she came to hear of it, and was furious because it meant they might become available to Greene's biographer, Norman Sherry. He had been altogether too open about Catherine Walston, and she was anxious to avoid the same exposure.

Catherine Crompton Walston was born in America, to an American mother and English father, and brought up in comfortable circumstances. By her teens she had become a drop-dead beauty, unconventional and unfettered.

At eighteen she met Harry Walston, a buttoned up but suitably eligible English bachelor, and the couple became engaged within three days. By the time of the wedding, she had already decided that she did not love him. She married him anyway. Unsurprisingly, relations soon broke down emotionally and sexually, but Harry adored her and accepted her regular affairs, in the hope that they would be discreetly conducted. They weren't, and Catherine (by then Lady Walston) acquired a racy reputation: Malcolm Muggeridge referred to her as 'sans merci but *so* belle'.

Twelve years into the marriage, Catherine set her

sights on Graham Greene, whose novels had prompted in her a desire to convert to Catholicism. In 1946, Catherine wrote to the novelist to ask if he would become her godfather – a relationship that must later have carried some perverse erotic charge. I rather suspect she intended this from the start. The priest who received her into the Church remembered her well: 'she was determined not to be chaste and yet she was deeply religious.' He did not add, though the thought must have crossed his mind: here was a perfect mate for Graham Greene.

Greene acceded, but sent his wife Vivien to the ceremony in which Catherine was received into the Church. From all surviving accounts, Vivien took against her new step-God-daughter from the beginning. Too rich, too chic, too sexy. 'I think,' Vivien remembered, 'she was out to get him. I think it was a quite straightforward grab.'

It wasn't difficult: Greene was there to be grabbed, and did most of the chasing. Like all *femmes fatales*, Catherine was remarkably good at making it clear that she needed (and loved) him less than he needed and loved her. Though the couple spent a lot of time together, at first at a simple romantic hideaway in Ireland, and later in Anacapri, Greene never felt entirely secure in the relationship. Catherine took other occasional lovers and, in response to Greene's jealousy, merely remarked that she would have no objection if he did so too. Catherine's Catholicism provided reason for remorse about the affair – a remorse that would have heightened the passion at the same time as it may have been undermining its foundations.

None of this can have made Greene entirely easy in the relationship. Catherine was free-spirited and sexually compelling in ways that neither Vivien nor Dorothy could have begun to compete with, and he became increasingly obsessed by her. Besotted, abandoning his young family, Greene made an easy target for those left behind. 'Until he met Mrs Walston,' Vivien recalled, 'he was always very sweet . . . He turned into a different person. She was a very bad influence on him – he became indifferent to the children and had furious and terrible tempers.' Well, she would say so, wouldn't she? But Hugh, Greene's brother, agreed entirely. Catherine came between him and Graham as well: 'she didn't take to me nor I to her,' he observed. 'Graham became harder then and less friendly. It was all Catherine Walston's fault.'

Like most such affairs, the end lies in the beginning, and it was likely that the relationship would eventually burn out. Catherine frequently tried to end the relationship, and when Greene was away, she would go on retreats to seek guidance and comfort. This threatened and alarmed the absent Greene, who once wrote: 'I love you & trust you & hope the priests & the shits won't work on you when I'm away.' But the priests and the shits, as he called them, were agents of conscience, freely chosen. It was only a matter of time before things fell apart. Significantly, by this time, he was, he confessed to his mother, tired of Anacapri, and ready to sell the Villa Rosaio. Ready, symbolically, to move on. The Rosaio Press would issue no more small volumes.

Within four years, Catherine had had enough. Greene wanted to carry on, even, half-heartedly, proposing marriage in 1951. But the combination of Catherine's growing doubts, and her husband's ultimatum that she give up her lover, hastened the end. In March, as a parting gift, Greene wistfully sent Catherine the manuscript of *The End of the Affair*: 'I love you and bastard that I am, I'm married to you by this ms. Graham. Put up with me for another year or two.'

It is from that excellent novel that we know the story of Bendrix and Sarah – immediately identifiable in literary London as Greene and Walston – and it provides a pretty reliable guide to what went on. Unlike *After Two Years*, it was widely distributed, and though Catherine bore the exposure both bravely and proudly, her family – and Greene's – were humiliated and enraged by it. From their point of view it would have been better to have been privately printed, and its distribution withheld, like *After Two Years*. But while the suppression of the latter was sensible, and no loss to literature, the novel deserved publication, even at the expense of the hurt it caused. The people on whose lives it painfully drew are all dead now, but the novel continues to delight its new generations of readers. It is, unsurprisingly, a particular favourite of women readers – a fact that Greene wryly acknowledged in his inscription to my own copy of the book, describing it as 'the book which women like'.

In August of 1994, I produced a little pamphlet – in celebration of my birthday – elegantly printed by Sebastian Carter at the Rampant Lions Press, entitled *Gekoski: The First Fifty Years*. Limited (naturally) to 50 copies, for my friends and family, the text consisted of a set of random aperçus and frivolities, which even I have no desire to reissue in this, or any other, context. Writing and distributing it made sense at that particular time; it amused me a lot and my friends a little, and it was never intended for wider distribution. I never thought of it as a book: rather, as a printed gift. In the same way, I suspect, Graham Greene would have resisted the notion that *After Two Years* was one of his books, part of the corpus of his work, rather than of the texture of his life. It is only the sad assiduousness of the pedant that rescues such works, and tries to make of them something more than was ever intended by the author. Neither Greene's bibliographer, nor his biographer, not even the august *CBEL*, saw fit to mention Greene's private little pamphlet of poems to his lover. It rather embarrasses me to have told you about it, but it was irresistible: I know about it, and you (presumably) didn't.

ANIMAL FARM

The English satirical magazine, *Private Eye*, has a column called 'Pseud's Corner' which prints pretentious snippets garnered from the previous week's publications. I have only been cited in it once, from my Catalogue Number 3, item 124 (issued in 1983) describing a letter of George Orwell's. The letter read: 'Dear Sir, I have only just received your letter dated October 11, which had to be forwarded to me. Since you ask for a copy of my signature here it is. Yours truly, Geo. Orwell.' It sold for £275 ($500), which wasn't much, since Orwell letters, though uncommon, tend to be business-like. Hence my catalogue description (quoted in full in *Private Eye*): 'The letter, though terse to the point of self-extinction, seems to me characteristically Orwellian.'

It is presumably some confirmation of the fact that I *am* a Pseud, that this still seems to me a snappy little observation. Orwell was reticent and courteous with strangers, though his letter suggests that these qualities were not unaccompanied by waspish pride. He disliked signing books or giving autographs, and was able to indicate this while in the very process of signing. In the world of rare books, his is an uncommon signature: in the following twenty years, I have handled only a couple of other Orwell letters, and a handful of inscribed copies of his books. Though uncommon, they are never easy to sell, because Orwell collectors tend to be more interested in books with dust jackets than in anything (if I might put it this way) *real*.

Of Orwell's works, *Nineteen Eighty Four* would appear to be the scarcest bearing an authorial inscription, as it was published only a few months before his death in January 1950. I am unaware of any copy on the open market in the last twenty-five years, and can trace only one example, in the School Library at Eton College, which is inscribed to Rayner Heppenstall. If another copy, with a similarly good association, were to come on the market, I have no doubt that it would fetch £30,000 ($54,000). (A nice dustwrappered first edition is worth, say, £3,000 ($5,400).)

The equally celebrated *Animal Farm* (1945), on the other hand, is more common inscribed. Only 4,500 copies were printed initially, followed two weeks later by another 10,000. We have handled four inscribed copies, of which one (to Malcolm Muggeridge) was a first edition, and three (including one to Arthur Koestler) were second impressions. Surprisingly, this neat little satire on the excesses of Soviet communism, which had been turned down by so many publishers that Orwell had considered publishing it himself, became his first bestseller. When it was published in America, in 1946, the print run was 50,000, and within four years it had sold over half a million copies.

His novels in the 1930s, beginning with *Down and Out in Paris and London* (1930), had sold modestly, and Orwell had established himself as a clear-eyed commentator on the social conditions in a variety of places, ranging from Kent to Burma to Catalonia. The books were crisply written and observed, intelligent and demanding in their sympathies, though limited somewhat by the fact that his characters always seemed a function of the conditions that produced them. Though I admire his work greatly, I never feel that he is, quite, a novelist. Rather, some intelligent hybrid operating between the genres of autobiography, journalism and prose fiction. His publishing history in this period bears this out. Prior to the publication of *Animal Farm*, Orwell had not published a novel for six years, concentrating instead on his work at the BBC and as literary editor of *Tribune*, and on producing essays and reviews on a wide range of political and literary topics.

When the desire to write fiction returned, late in 1943, it was not a novel he contemplated but a short fable featuring barnyard animals, led by highly intelligent pigs, who take over their farm and run it as a socialist collective.

The book took only a few months to write, during which Orwell described it to a friend as 'a little squib which might amuse you when it comes out.' But, as he anticipated, it took some time to find a publisher. Victor Gollancz, who had published most of Orwell's previous works, and had a contractual right to his next two novels, disliked the book's palpable anti-Stalinism. 'We couldn't have published it then,' Gollancz later remarked. 'Those people were fighting for us and had just saved our necks at Stalingrad.' He declined the book immediately, as did Jonathan Cape and Nicolson & Watson.

In June, Orwell sent the manuscript, which had been scorched and crumpled when a bomb hit the Orwells' flat in Mortimer Crescent, to T.S. Eliot at Faber and Faber, with the following comment:

> If you read this MS yourself you will see its meaning which is not an acceptable one at this moment . . . Cape or the MOI [Ministry of Information] made the imbecile suggestion that some animal other than pigs might be made to represent the Bolsheviks. I could not of course make any change of that description.

Eliot agreed entirely: drop the pigs? Ridiculous. What Orwell had to do, he argued, was change their *nature.* He admired the book, but doubted its politics: 'Your pigs are far more intelligent than the other animals, and therefore best qualified to run the farm . . . What was needed (some might argue) was not more communism but more public-spirited pigs.'

Michael Shelden, one of Orwell's biographers, believes that Eliot 'completely missed the point of the book', which, if true, must be something of a first. In fact, Eliot's comment obliquely got to the very heart of the matter: in Orwell's view, there should be no ruler-animals, and the turning point in *Animal Farm* comes when the other, stupider, animals allow the more intelligent pigs special privileges and eventual ascendancy over them. Until then, when the farm first becomes an egalitarian collective: 'the animals were happy as they had never conceived it possible to be. Every mouthful of food was an acute positive pleasure, now it was truly their own food, produced by themselves and for themselves, not doled out to them by a grudging master.' So Paradise on earth can be achieved, however briefly.

In Eliot's view, however, it is no use trusting the workings of egalitarian socialism, which gives equal power to the intelligent pig and the willing, but stupid, sheep. Instead, it is the primary task of a culture to locate powerfully capable and benevolent figures, and to be guided by them. Thus the fault of the animals lies in choosing Snowball (the committee-forming

Trotsky) and the ruthless Napoleon (Stalin) rather than some alternative 'public-spirited' pigs. Whether pigs are capable of such benevolence, and how to choose the ones that are, would appear to be the issue.

Dispirited, Orwell soon wrote to his literary agent, Leonard Moore, to say that he was contemplating publishing the book himself as a pamphlet at two shillings. His sole remaining hope was that Fred Warburg, who had published *Homage to Catalonia* in 1938, might agree to publish the book. Warburg was more sympathetic to the politics of *Animal Farm* than Victor Gollancz, and quickly agreed to publish, subject to finding an adequate supply of paper. By the beginning of October, the paper found, publisher and writer had agreed terms, without the need of a written contract. Orwell received an advance of £88 ($160).

The publication process was uncommonly slow, especially for such a short book (which ran to ninety-two pages in the first edition). As Orwell was fully aware, Warburg was stalling until the war ended, when a book containing a radical attack on a crucial ally would no longer cause outrage. In a spirit of conciliation, Orwell used the delay to make one important change in the text:

In Chapter VIII (I think it is VIII) when the windmill is blown up, I wrote 'all the animals including Napoleon flung themselves to their faces.' I would

like to alter it to 'all the animals except Napoleon.'
. . . I just thought the alteration would be fair to JS,
as he did stay in Moscow during the German
advance.

In its particulars, then, *Animal Farm* is explicitly
intended as an attack on Russian communism. But it
has, Orwell insisted, more general interest. He
conceived the fable as an attack on 'the gramophone
mind' – the capacity of people and cultures to be hood-
winked and dominated by slogans and political rhet-
oric. Any culture, he observed, could fall prey to the
process of indoctrination through mass-stupidity. It is
essential to resist the process 'whether or not one agrees
with the record that is being played at the moment'.

It is a nice irony that the target of the satire, then,
is not merely Stalinist Russia, but many of his readers
as well. For a generation of English socialists in the
1930s, Russia had been a beacon of hope for social
and economic equality. It is astonishing, in retrospect,
how gullible the middle-class communists of the thirties were: how comprehensively they swallowed the
phoney Russian statistics about their economic mira-
cles, how passively they toured Russia, accepting what
they were shown, and given.

Animal Farm makes the point explicitly, in Squealer's
ability to hoodwink the gullible, starving animals:

Reading out the figures in a shrill, rapid voice, he proved to them in detail that they had more oats, more hay, more turnips than they had in Jones's day, that they worked shorter hours, that their drinking water was of better quality, that they lived longer . . .

Like the animals, the English socialists of the thirties 'believed every word of it': of the success of the communist revolution, and the moral superiority of the Russian model over the capitalist one. They seemed incapable, in spite of growing evidence, of recognizing the brutality of a regime under which fifteen million people had died through collectivization, purges and gulags.

But in spite of the wide range of its satire, *Animal Farm* received surprisingly good reviews, and sold exceptionally well. Clearly, the decision to construct his political critique as a fable had been a wise one. As a form, an allegory using animals simplifies, generalizes and expands the potential readership, making otherwise unpalatable or uninteresting truths both immediate and, in this case, positively charming. The book, elegantly written, and with more wit than one associates with Orwell's other work, delighted a public which would never have considered reading a political tract on the same subject. Even Eliot, though he had no desire to publish, had to concede that 'the fable is very skilfully handled, and the narrative keeps one's interest on its own plane – and that is something very few authors have achieved since Gulliver.'

Orwell rarely commented publicly on his own work. But in the case of *Animal Farm* he made an exception, and he made it in a characteristically quirky fashion. When the first Ukrainian translation of the book, *Kolgosp Tvarin*, was published in 1947, Orwell used the occasion to append a Preface, in which he described his desire to uncover 'the negative influence of the Soviet myth upon the western Socialist movement'. (Why Ukrainians alone deserved such an explanation is never made clear.) He reminded his readers (his *Ukrainian* readers?) that there was a specific political point to all this farmyard stuff:

I do not wish to comment on the work; if it does not speak for itself, it is a failure. But I should like to emphasise two points: first, that although the various episodes are taken from the actual history of the Russian Revolution, they are dealt with schematically and their chronological order is changed . . . The second point has been missed by most critics, possibly because I did not emphasise it sufficiently. A number of readers may finish the book with the impression that it ends in the complete reconciliation of the pigs and the humans. That was not my intention; on the contrary I wrote it immediately after the Teheran Conference which everybody thought had established the best possible relations between the USSR and the West . . . I personally did not believe that such good relations would last long; and, as events have shown, I wasn't far wrong.

I've always been rather surprised that this Ukrainian edition of *Animal Farm* isn't more highly sought after by Orwell collectors. Over the years I have handled a couple of copies, and never charged more than £125 ($225) for them, in spite of the fact that they are much scarcer than the English first edition (which can fetch up to £3,000 ($5,400) in fine condition). On the internet at the moment, there is only one copy of the Ukrainian edition listed (at $300), and over twenty first editions of the English issue, all of which cost more than that. And, in spite of the fact that the internet *Kolgosp Tvarin* is a fine copy, I'm not buying it for stock. Orwell collectors, not that there are many of them, are an unimaginative bunch, and resist bibliographic oddities. You might assume that some enterprising librarian would buy it, but given that the Preface is reprinted in Orwell's *Collected Essays, Journalism, and Letters*, even the collecting institutions don't want it.

My friend the publisher, author and collector Tom Rosenthal does, however, own the Ukrainian edition, and (he points out proudly) an unrecorded Latvian translation as well. As the latter is not listed in the bibliography, he has bequeathed it to the Orwell Archive at University College, London. A noble exception to my intemperate dismissal of Orwell collectors as mere fetishists, he is also the happy possessor of Fred Warburg's own copy of *Animal Farm*, signed by Orwell. I've been trying to get it off him for years, but (sensibly enough) he's not selling.

Sadly, there aren't many single-author collectors any more. As recently, say, as twenty years ago, there were a considerable number of collectors who wanted to own everything a writer had produced: books, contributions to books and periodicals, ephemeral bits and pieces. Some of these obsessives even collected translations and later printings of the books of their favourite authors. And to this, if you had the means and taste, might be added manuscripts and letters by, even about, the author, and copies of books from his library. It was a labour of love, and much more consuming a project than simply trawling about for perfect copies of the most famous books: a search for the scarce rather than the rare, for research interest rather than fetishistic or financial value.

Orwell is a nice example of an author who ought to be collected in depth, because so much of his work was done in newspapers, small magazines, and broadcasts for the BBC. This has been wonderfully described by Gillian Fenwick in the standard Orwell bibliography, but I know of no collector who has the means, the vision, and the patience (much less the shelf space) to attempt the task of making a really comprehensive Orwell collection. It's a shame. It would be more fun than paying large sums to upgrade one's copies into nicer dustwrappers, and it would make a collection that, if kept together, would be a valuable resource for scholars. Book collecting doesn't have to be a mere form of acquisitiveness and investment. It can involve connoisseurship: the scholarly, creative and useful putting together of objects both compelling in themselves and of interest to others. To do this you need to know a lot, and have a fine capacity to discriminate. Rare qualities, these days.

THE SATANIC VERSES

In general, a bookseller's life is a happy, peaceful and orderly one. We live like emperors of Lilliputian kingdoms, crusty but benign, remarkably unbuffeted by intrusions of anything unpleasantly resembling reality. Adventures are limited to those of the trade, and the relative lack of excitement is compensated for by ease of life, the congeniality of the books, and the company of other booksellers and collectors. So it came as something of a surprise to me to be included in the Fatwa that was issued against Salman Rushdie.

I suppose there was some danger in my publishing project at the time, for my Sixth Chamber Press was in the process of printing a new book of Rushdie's entitled *Two Stories*. One of which, entitled 'The Prophet's Hair', is, I am told (I am no student of such things) of questionable piety, fundamentally considered. As far as I know, however, news of this obscure volume never reached Teheran. The sluggish sales of its 72 copies were never such as to suggest that it had penetrated English consciousness, much less Iranian.

But I had a small role to play in the publication of *The Satanic Verses*, and it was specified that such persons were to be included in the death threat issued against Rushdie. On 14 February 1989, the Ayatollah Khomeini, as the spiritual guide of Shia Muslims, had issued an unambiguous edict:

> I would like to inform all the intrepid Muslims in the world that the author of the book *The Satanic Verses*, which has been compiled, printed and published in opposition to Islam, the Prophet and the Koran, as well as those publishers who were aware of its contents, have been sentenced to death. I call on all zealous Muslims to execute them quickly . . .'

Though its author remained unscathed, the book's Italian translator and Norwegian publisher were subsequently attacked, and its Japanese translator murdered, so I presumably had some slight cause for alarm.

The Fatwa was a response to the violence caused by the book's publication, not its cause. The chronology is instructive. Following the book's publication in England on 26 September 1988, it was banned in India on 5 October, in South Africa on 24 November, and then in Pakistan, Saudi Arabia, Egypt,

Somalia, Bangladesh, Sudan, Malaysia, Indonesia and Qatar. *The Satanic Verses* was publicly incinerated in Bradford on 14 January, and widely denounced by Muslim clerics throughout Britain, culminating in a demonstration in Hyde Park on 27 January. 'How fragile civilization is; how easily, how merrily a book burns!' observed Rushdie sadly. On 12 February in Islamabad, five people died during riots protesting about the novel. The Fatwa was issued two days later.

How much of this was predictable? Apparently one of the publisher's readers had predicted that if the book was published there would be 'blood in the streets', but I do not believe that anyone at Viking could have foreseen the reaction. Even Rushdie, who was aware – and intended – that the book would be controversial, was astonished by the violence of the opposition. *The Satanic Verses* was vilified in the Muslim world, but not widely read. Passages from the book were excerpted, cheaply printed, and distributed in the mosques in order to inflame feeling. In one, which was regarded as particularly offensive, a character has lewd dreams about the prophet's wives. Rushdie replied reasonably that such passages had to be read in context. The book, considered as a whole, was respectful but not uncritical.

It didn't wash, and for the first time the Western world became the theatre for acts of violence emanating from the Middle East. After the offices of

Viking were bombed, the publishers suspended plans for the paperback edition, which Rushdie regarded as a betrayal, but which was astonishingly supported by writers as diverse as John le Carré, Roald Dahl, John Berger and Norman Podhoretz. Eventually Penguin paperbacks of the book, which were first made available at the Frankfurt Book Fair in 1988, began to be distributed in Switzerland, but they were soon withdrawn. These copies now fetch more in the rare book market – up to £200 ($360) – than do the genuine first editions, which are common enough, and still cheap at £75 ($135). A mass market paperback edition was finally issued in 1992 by 'The Consortium', a conglomerate of several unspecified publishing houses, operating under an unbombable imprint that, like Rushdie, had no fixed abode.

Rushdie knew he had written an inflammatory book, and he stood by it. He regretted the deaths and protests, but he didn't regret writing and publishing the book. But he had made the Faustian choice, however unwittingly. Famously ambitious, he got everything he had dreamt of: he was suddenly the most discussed, the most controversial, the best known author in the world. It was hard to avoid the conclusion that his fate suited him.

I saw a lot of him in the next few years, and came to admire him greatly. There was something childlike and pure in his self-absorption, nothing neurotic in his egoism – he had a self worth being absorbed in. His confidence was undiminished by his cares, and he was always good value to listen to, and argue with. The monarchy would be disestablished within ten years; Angela Carter was a major novelist; film was as significant a university subject as literature. These were, I argued, idiotic notions. He snorted: these weren't opinions, they were facts.

Over the next years, he paid a heavy price. His wife, the novelist Marianne Wiggins, left him, his privacy and freedom were brutally diminished, and he was called upon to defend himself against a variety of attacks, most of them hostile, ignorant and ill-expressed. In 1990 he announced that he had 'embraced Islam', though he later recanted. It was, he later admitted, a bad idea. People of genius frequently have poor judgement. Following the inner voice doesn't necessarily give you any sense.

To a secular Westerner it was hard to imagine not defending Rushdie's right to publish as he wished, though many of his supporters wished *The Satanic Verses* had been a better book. When I belatedly began to read it, I was greeted by an opening scene in which, after an explosion on a plane, two characters float down to earth singing songs, and land safely (as an angel and a devil) in London. You could hardly imagine anything less congenial to me. I hate magic realism, its attempt to assimilate the imaginative freedom of the fairy tale to the more constricted domain of the novel.

Like many readers, I never finished *The Satanic Verses*. On every page I found something to admire: an aperçu, a fabulously wrought phrase, an odd angle of vision that made me smile. It had genius, but there was something unrelentingly same-y about the prose, and the succession of scenes, that made me feel that, after a few hundred pages, I'd had enough. I wasn't disappointed exactly, just prematurely satisfied.

Sometime after Rushdie signed the contract with Viking to produce the book, and many months before the Fatwa craziness, his publisher Tony Lacey had decided that it might be profitable and amusing to produce a signed, limited edition alongside the trade version of the book. But Lacey had never done such an edition before, nor had any of Rushdie's books been so issued, though this is now a regular occurrence.

'How,' Lacey asked his author, 'does one go about such a thing?'

'Ask Rick,' replied Salman, as we were in the process of discussing the publication of *Two Stories*, and the question of print runs and prices for limited editions was fresh in our respective minds. He'd been a pleasure to deal with, and his unjustly earned reputation for greediness (he'd just changed publishers and signed a big new contract) was belied by his conduct. I had told him that my Sixth Chamber Press simply paid whatever an author asked. Rightly enough, he looked puzzled.

'How much did John Updike get?' (I had just published Updike's *The Afterlife*.)

'Five hundred dollars.'

He thought for a while.

'Can I have $500 too?'

'Sure,' I said. He was fun to work with, and wanted to have a say in choosing the typeface and binding, and arranging the illustrations with Bhupen Khakar. He was delighted with the result, in its beautiful binding by Romilly Saumerez Smith, because it was the only one of his books that he had designed himself.

A few weeks later, having lunch with Gillon Aitken, Rushdie's estimably ferocious agent, I conveyed the terms of the agreement I had reached with Salman. I'd never seen Gillon go entirely silent before, but he quickly recovered himself, demanding extra author's copies of the book on behalf of his client. I agreed, and the colour returned to his cheeks.

When Tony Lacey rang to discuss production of the Viking edition, I suggested that he 'obey the Law of Private Press Issuance'.

'What's that?'

'"You can't print too few, you can't charge too much." Keep the print run small, and make them a bit expensive. The market can always assimilate a few signed copies of an important book by an important writer.'

'How few, how much?'

'Well,' I said, 'they will be ugly – no commercial publisher can produce a decent-looking signed, limited edition. Yours will be like the rest: in some cheap leather binding round the ordinary trade edition. So you can't go wild on pricing. But I think you could get away with 100 copies in quarter leather at, say, £60 ($110) each, and an extra 12 in full leather at £150 ($270).'

'Excellent,' he said, totally uninterested in the frankness of my opinions, 'we'll do it.'

'Do you want to know how much my advice on the matter has cost you?' I asked.

'No . . .' he said, a little warily. No mention of a consultancy fee had been made.

'I get all twelve of the extra specials at trade price.'

The phone went that little bit quiet at the other end, and I was expecting to be told where to get off.

'Wonderful,' he said, sounding quite relieved. I had forgotten that publishers of new books actually like selling them, whereas your average rare book dealer disgorges the better books from his stock reluctantly, wondering, with every occasional sale, whether the book, since it sold, wasn't too cheap.

'Wait a minute,' he added after a little thought. 'Shouldn't Salman get Number 1?'

'Seems fair enough,' I said, a trifle reluctantly, having envisaged ownership of the book myself. (But Copy Number II he inscribed: 'To Rick, this copy no.

II from the owner of no. I – Best wishes, Salman Rushdie.')

Almost no one, on the book's publication in 1988, could have foreseen its quite extraordinary future, and the retrospectively modest prices of the limited edition were, in the light of Rushdie's reputation at the time, reasonable, maybe even a bit cheeky. Within a few months, however, the 100 copies were changing hands at £250 ($450), and the 10 copies, which I had placed with selected friends and customers, were fetching well over £1,000 each. I bought four of them back, one from Ted Hughes, who could never resist a decent profit.

According to reports in the media, following the Fatwa, Rushdie 'went into hiding', a phrase that now seems more appropriate to a mole or Saddam Hussein, and did not accurately describe the peripatetic and secretive existence that was forced upon him. In fact, Salman, though he had to make himself scarce and was under constant police protection, kept in pretty good touch with his friends, and continued to lead a modified version of that frenetic social life that has always characterized him. Certainly, it was no problem for him to get to my launch party for the publication of *Two Stories*. In a short speech designed to welcome him, I alluded to a recent incident that had happened to me, and which, I felt, must reveal the pressure that Rushdie had been under for many months. Only a few days after the publication of *Two Stories*, *The Independent* ran a front-page story about the book. Though it did not name the publisher (in any case, no one has heard of my Sixth Chamber Press), the article went so far as to suggest that Rushdie was unrepentantly publishing yet another dangerous story, and that some damn fool was mad, or bold, enough to publish it.

My wife and children were furious with me for going ahead with publication, but I wasn't much worried about it – presumably the hunt for the infidel Rushdie was unlikely to be deflected in my direction. Three days later, I was driving back to Warwickshire, up the Finchley Road, listening to the Test Match, and reflecting quietly on a most interesting week. All of a sudden, the cricket went off the air, to be replaced by a voice speaking (aggressively) in German. I stopped the car abruptly, and horns began to blare.

I don't know very much about how radio waves are transmitted and received, or the wiring of cars, but something puzzling and sinister was going on. The conclusion was obvious: someone had put either a bomb or a small Nazi in my car. I got out, as the blaring of the horns multiplied, and opened the bonnet, peering into the engine with increasing anxiety.

A bomb? A bomb? I looked about anxiously, and had seen nothing alarming when it occurred to me that I was looking for one of those round black things with a fuse, like in Tom and Jerry, that says BOMB in white letters. None of those . . . Doing my natural childbirth deep breathing, and starting to drool a little, I redefined my notions, and wiped my chin. A bomb was something cylindrical and metallic, with wires coming out of it, right? I looked back in, and suddenly there were dozens of suspicious objects in there. Presumably some were carburettors or sparking plugs, but I don't know what they look like either. Bombs, lots of bombs.

There were two clear choices: abandon the car in the middle of the Finchley Road, in the middle of rush hour, and run like hell, screaming 'Bomb! Bomb!' Or get back in the car and face the music. Being pretty assimilated to English ways after twenty-five years, I opted for the latter: rather risk immediate, violent dismemberment than cause a scene. Anyway, if I died it would be quick, and my children might eventually remember me as something of a martyr. Maybe even a hero.

I closed the bonnet, got back in the car, and started the engine. After a few moments of blissfully ongoing life, I decided to take the ultimate gamble, and switch the radio back on.

'We apologize,' the voice of Christopher Martin-Jenkins said soothingly, 'for the break in transmission of the cricket, which was caused by a fault in our transmitters.'

As I told the story, the small audience gathered round in my flat gave a slight collective chuckle, which sounded sympathetic to me. Turning to Salman, I said, 'I mention this because it gave me some small insight of how great the pressures on you have been, and how frightening they must be.'

He considered this carefully. 'Not at all,' said Salman, 'I have never been frightened for a single moment. All it shows is what a coward you are.'

POEMS (1919)

If this delicate little volume didn't have a printed label on it, you could mistake it for a painting. I suppose that's because it is a painting, and by no less an artist than Roger Fry, who hand-made the marbled paper in which it's covered. It's an exuberant abstract design in swirling yellows, oranges and browns, all mixed up together, onto which a bright green has been allowed to drip, as in a painting by Jackson Pollock. It's gorgeous, ravishing, my second favourite book of the twentieth century. The printed label, though, reveals the object for what it really is. A bound volume of a few pages entitled *Poems* by T.S. Eliot. It was hand-printed and published in 1919 by Virginia and Leonard Woolf at the Hogarth Press.

So attractive is the book that it had a place of honour in a vitrine at the Tate Gallery exhibition 'The Art of Bloomsbury', 1999. The curator of that show, the art historian Richard Shone, is a great admirer of the design:

If you run your finger very carefully over it, (you're not allowed to though) you'll feel it's got a texture to it, where the paint has thickened or thinned and I think it's simply a brush or a sponge perhaps swept across the paper. I think it's very beautiful. I think it's one of the prettiest books of the early Hogarths.

The first book of the Woolf's Hogarth Press was published in 1917, but we have to go back a couple of years in order to understand how it all began. There is a revealing entry in Virginia Woolf's diary, for 25 January 1915 (her birthday):

And let me count up all the things I had. L[eonard] had sworn he would give me nothing, like a good wife I believed him, but he crept into my bed with a little parcel which was a beautiful green purse. And he brought breakfast with a paper, which announced a naval victory, and a square brown parcel with *The Abbot* in it, a lovely first edition. I was then taken up to town, free of charge and given a treat, first at a picture palace, and then at Buzzards. Sitting at tea, we decided three things. In the first place to take Hogarth [House], if we can get it, in the second to buy a printing press, in the third to buy a bulldog, probably called John. I'm very much excited at the idea of all three, particularly the press.

What a lot of treats. The phenomenally attentive
Leonard Woolf was, one recognizes, trying to inter-
vene in one of Virginia's frequent nervous collapses.
She'd just finished *The Voyage Out* (her first novel), and
the war was a constant torment to her. And so her
husband was deploying all of the trusted remedies for
depression: move house, develop a new hobby, work
with your hands, buy a puppy. The house, a handsome Georgian residence in Richmond was duly
rented. The printing press agreed upon, though the
actual object didn't appear for two more years. I don't
know what happened about the puppy. Presumably
it's not that easy to buy a bulldog called John.

The printing press was delayed on grounds of cost:
'As the press cost £20 and we're rather hard-up just
now, I'm afraid we shall have to wait to buy it until
March.' And in the middle of March, according to
Leonard, they got lucky:

On March 23rd 1917 we were walking one afternoon up Farringdon Street from Fleet Street to
Holborn Viaduct when we passed the Excelsior
Printing Supply Company. It's not a very large firm,
but it sold every kind of printing machine and material from a hand press and type to a composing
stick. Nearly all the implements of printing are
materially attractive and we stared through the
window at them like two hungry children gazing at

buns and cakes in a baker shop window. We went in and explained our desire and dilemma to a very sympathetic man in a brown overall. He was extremely encouraging.

This obliging salesman provided the Woolfs with a printing press, type, chases, cases, and a pamphlet that he said would 'infallibly' teach them how to print. The pamphlet did indeed teach them how to print, but it was hardly infallible. Eventually, after a year or so of frustrating trial and error, Virginia began to get the hang of it.

One has great blocks of type, which have to be divided into their separate letters and fonts, and then put into the right partitions, the work of ages, especially when you mix the 'h's with the 'n's as I did yesterday. We get so absorbed, we can't stop. I see that real printing will devour one's entire life.

The work of setting type and binding volumes was therapeutic for Virginia, because it took her away from the imaginative stress of literary composition. Becoming a semi-professional printer was not only agreeable, it even began to make a little money. Leonard was an extremely meticulous businessman, who counted the pennies, and liked the whole technical, practical side of their new enterprise. He too had a sort of nervous quality in his make-up, which found great tranquillity in stacking up the volumes he'd stitched or printed.

Most days found Virginia calmly setting type, getting quicker, more accurate, and more aesthetically assured: 'Wednesday 10th April 1918. A very wet, dark day. Printed. I set up one page in one hour and fifteen minutes, my record.' That afternoon, the Woolfs were visited by Miss Harriet Weaver, proprietor of *The Egoist* magazine, who wished to know if the Hogarth Press might care to publish Mr James Joyce's *Ulysses*. 'Which,' according to Virginia, 'no other printer will do, owing presumably to its sentiments, they must be very warm, considering the success he had with his last.'

Miss Weaver had the manuscript with her, and for the next year it was to reside at the Woolfs' as they sought a commercial printer who might be willing to take the job on. They certainly couldn't do it themselves, because at Virginia's rate of page setting, I calculate it would have taken just over forty-seven years for them to produce a final text.

Eventually, as we know, the book was published in Paris in 1922, by Sylvia Beach. Bound in blue covers, which Joyce insisted had to match the colour of the Greek flag, *Ulysses* is a majestic object, certainly my favourite book of the twentieth century. But if the Hogarth Press had just missed out on an opportunity to publish a high priest of the modern movement, they were soon to enlist the services of another.

Friday 15th November, 1918. I was interrupted somewhere on this page by the arrival of Mr Eliot. Mr Eliot is well expressed by his name. A polished, cultivated, elaborate young American, talking so slow that each word seems to have special finish allotted it. But beneath the surface it is fairly evident that he is very intellectual, intolerant, with strong views of his own, and a poetic creed. He produced three or four poems for us to look at, the fruit of two years, since he works all day in a bank, and in his reasonable way, thinks regular work good for people of nervous constitutions.

The nervous Mr Eliot and the depressive Mrs Woolf had met at just the right moment. She needed new writers and he needed a new publisher. Eliot's *Prufrock and Other Observations*, now recognized as one of the great books of the century, had come out the previous year, but hadn't been very favourably received. The following was typical:

Mr Eliot is one of those clever young men who find it amusing to pull the leg of a sober reviewer: 'I'll just put down the first thing that comes into my head and call it *The Love Song of J. Alfred Prufrock*'.

We do not wish to appear patronising, but we are certain Mr Eliot could do finer work on traditional lines. With him it seems to be a case of missing the effect by too much cleverness.

Nobody likes a smart ass, especially one *that* smart. But Mrs Woolf, who was tolerably clever herself, was sympathetic: 'Eliot has sent us some of his poems, which we're going to print as soon as *Kew Gardens* is done.'

The poems which Eliot was offering were unrelentingly modern: knowing, crisp, ironic, alternating between low vernacular and high academic, *and* in both French and English. Consider their titles: 'Sweeney amongst the Nightingales', 'The Hippopotamus', 'Mélange adultère de tout'. The opening lines of 'Mr Eliot's Sunday Morning Service' establish the tone:

> Polyphiloprogenitive
> The sapient sutlers of the Lord
> Drift across the window-panes.
> In the beginning was the Word.
>
> In the beginning was the Word.
> Superfetation of τό ἕν,
> And at the mensual turn of time
> Produced enervate Origen.

You hardly know which to turn to first, your dictionary or your aspirins. Seven obscure words in only eight lines? Even my spell-checker doesn't know five of them. This was other, and more, than what had previously been regarded as poetry. You couldn't just enjoy and understand it, you had to solve it first. If *Prufrock* had engendered hostility, this book was likely to enrage.

Viewed with hindsight, the resulting book is a perfect marriage of form and content, a modernist painting enclosing a radical new poetic voice. You might argue *Poems* is one of the key texts in the emergence of English modernism. But from the point of view of the protagonists, there was no sense of being at a critical moment of literary history, there was simply a book to be produced. What the Woolfs were really worried about was getting the colour of the binding right, and that turned out to be more a matter of luck than of judgement.

According to Richard Shone, the use of different coloured papers was not exactly arbitrary, but had large elements of chance: 'they would either buy them at a shop, or Roger Fry or another of their artist friends would paint large sheets of paper, which they would then cut and fold for the covers and stick on the titles.'

The Woolfs always consulted their authors about the design and binding of the books, and Eliot was pleased by their suggestions:

Dear Mrs Woolf,

Thank you so much for sending me the patterns and so many of them. I still think the one originally chosen is the best and would probably also be best liked by the people that might buy the book. The dark blue one is also good, but these may be rather expensive, so I have chosen one of the others as an alternative and it is only reasonable to leave the choice between these three to you.

I think one should stress how extraordinary this little book would have looked in the equivalent of Waterstone's in 1919, if it was put on the shelf with all the latest volumes, which tended to be of a very discreet grey or dove blue colour, with rather old-fashioned italic lettering on them.

Though she had confidence in her young Mr Eliot, Virginia was uneasy about the forthcoming reception of his eye- and ear-catching new book.

12th May 1919. We are in the thick of our publishing season. [John Middleton] Murry, Eliot and myself are in the hands of the public this morning, for this reason, perhaps, I feel slightly, but decidedly depressed.

Sure enough, most of the reviewers didn't like the new book any better than they had liked *Prufrock*.

Arthur Clutton-Brock, writing in the *TLS*, hated it, and gave Mr Eliot a piece of his mind:

> Mr Eliot likes to display out of the way learning. He likes to surprise you with every trick he can think of. But poetry is a serious art, too serious for this game . . . He's in danger of becoming silly, and what will he do then? He is probably reacting against poetry like that of Mr Murry, but you cannot live on reactions, you must forget them and all the errors that the past writers have committed, you must be brave enough to risk some positive follies of your own, otherwise you will fall more and more into negative follies, you will bury your talent in a napkin and become an artist who never does anything but giggle faintly.

But if you really want to hear some faint giggling, note the following positive review, from *The Athenaeum*:

> Mr Eliot is certainly damned by his newness and strangeness, but those two qualities which in most art are completely unimportant, because ephemeral, in him claim the attention of even the serious critic, for they are part of the fabric of his poetry. Mr Eliot is always quite consciously trying for something, it's something which has grown out of and developed beyond all the poems of all the dead poets. The

cautious critic, warned by the lamentable record of his tribe, might avoid answering the question 'Is this poetry' by asking to see a little more of Mr Eliot than is shown in these seven short poems. But to tell the truth, seven poems reveal a great deal of any poet. There is poetry in Mr Eliot.

That may not sound funny in itself, but it gets distinctly amusing when you recognize that it was written by Leonard Woolf. He and Virginia had some compunction about whether this was entirely fair. So they decided that *she* would review Middleton Murry's book, and *he* would do Eliot's, as if two thieves had decided it would be morally preferable if one of them lifted the family silver, and the other carried it out of the window. In any case, Leonard Woolf was right. It was about time somebody said in print that Mr Eliot was a poet.

The Woolfs printed 250 copies of *Poems* and sold them out in a year. They cost 2/6d each, which seems cheap, but actually represented half a day's pay for a schoolteacher at the time. So in today's values, a copy of *Poems* might cost you £30 ($55) or £40 ($70). You'd be lucky. In fact, today one would cost you more like four or five months' wages.

I have never seen a copy of the book with a contemporary inscription by Eliot, and often wondered whether he gave one to the Woolfs, and (if so) where it now resides. He was a diffident young man, unwilling to draw attention to himself. But he did give Mrs Woolf a copy of his next book, *Poems* (1920) published by Alfred A. Knopf, his first collection of poetry published in America. I know where that one resides, because it is in my own collection. The inscription is modest ('Virginia Woolf from T.S. Eliot') and perfect.

I've had five uninscribed copies of *Poems* (1919) through my hands over the years, and the last one sold for £10,000 ($18,000). I remember each of them perfectly, one in red patterned cloth, one in blue, and three in very slightly different marbled papers. If I close my eyes, I can still visualize each one, and I still miss them, as if they were children I'd fostered, and then let go into the world.

HARRY POTTER AND THE PHILOSOPHER'S STONE

I've always wondered how King Midas did it. You know, touching things, and turning them into gold? Fabulous: you wake up, and with a flick of the finger it's instant riches. A golden toothbrush! A gold cereal spoon! You have to be careful, of course, not to hug the kids, or make love to the Queen. It's an enthralling idea, ridiculous, and dangerous. No one has ever explained quite how he did it. My theory is that he was clutching a philosopher's stone, which has a long reputation for accomplishing such transformations.

J.K. Rowling must have had a whole bag full. Because there's never been anything like Harry Potter in the world of publishing, or in the rare book market. The books and films have made Rowling one of the richest women in England, a fortune for her publishers, Bloomsbury and Scholastic, a multimillionaire of her literary agent, and a staggering amount of money for Warner Brothers Pictures. Even the designer of the book's front cover (it was issued without a dustwrapper) has cashed in to the tune of some £86,000 ($155,000) for the original artwork.

The story has been told so many times that it has become a sort of myth. The usual version has Joanne Rowling, an impoverished single mum living on the dole, driven by the icy cold from her unheated flat, writing away in a local café while her infant daughter sleeps by her side. The resulting manuscript is published to universal acclaim, and instant and unimaginable riches. Harry Potter joins Christopher Robin, Huckleberry Finn and Peter Pan in the Pantheon of children's fiction. Joanne Rowling moves into a mansion as big as Hogwart's, and gets to work on the next six Harry Potters.

Much of the above is not quite accurate, as we shall see, and as the bemused Rowling has observed:

It's true that I wrote in cafés with my daughter sleeping beside me. That sounds very romantic but it isn't at all romantic when you are living through it. The embroidery comes when they say 'well, her flat was unheated'. I wasn't in search of warmth. I was just in search of good coffee frankly, and not having to interrupt the flow by getting up and making myself more coffee.

No, she's not an impoverished proletarian scribbler, but a nice middle-class graduate (in French) from

Exeter University, who after a brief sojourn and marriage in Portugal, returned to Edinburgh with her new daughter, severely depressed, and wondering what to do next. Like many Arts graduates, she was trying her hand at a bit of fiction. She loved writing, and was good at it: she'd been doing it almost all of her life.

She wrote her first story, 'Rabbit', at the age of six.

I was the epitome of a bookish child – short and squat, thick National Health glasses, living in a world of complete daydreams, wrote stories endlessly and occasionally came out of the fog to bully my poor sister and force her to listen to my stories and play the games I'd invented.

It was in one of these daydreamy states, while riding on a train many years later, that Harry Potter just popped into her head. Gazing at the cows out of the window:

all of a sudden the idea for Harry just appeared in my mind's eye. I can't tell you why or what trig-gered it. But I saw the idea of Harry and the Wizard school very plainly. I suddenly had this basic idea of a boy who didn't know who he was, who didn't know he was a wizard until he got his invitation to wizard school. I have never been so excited by an idea.

Lacking pen and paper, she spent the whole journey thinking about the school and the people her hero (not yet named Harry Potter) would meet there. By the time the train arrived, she had created Ron Weasley, Hagrid the gamekeeper, and the ghosts Nearly Headless Nick and Peeves.

But a long period was to pass between conception and execution, as Rowling realized from the start that Harry was to be the hero not of a book, but of a series that would take him right through school. Since 1990 she has been working on all seven books at the same time. Apparently the final chapter of the final book was written quite early on, and then locked away in a drawer, as she works meticulously towards her preordained climax.

Having finished the first book in 1995, Rowling had no clear idea about how to get it published. A flick through the Yellow Pages located a literary agent called Christopher Little, whose name appealed to her, perhaps because it recalled the amiable talking mouse, Stuart Little. Or perhaps Christopher Robin? She sent off the manuscript, and (having worked briefly in publishing herself) settled down for the long wait.

Publishers and literary agents receive an astonishing number of unsolicited manuscripts, which tend to moulder in a pile, until some junior member of staff has a quick and sceptical look at them. In Mr Little's office, it was one Bryony Evens who first read *Harry*

Potter and the Philosopher's Stone, by the unknown Joanne Rowling. The agency did not normally handle children's books, but Evens, who loved them, 'read it rapidly because it was really so good, so funny, so brilliant'. She urged Christopher Little to consider it immediately and he read it overnight. He loved it too. Within a couple of months, after Rowling had agreed to a few minor changes, the manuscript was circulating amongst London's publishers.

But no one else thought much of it. Penguin turned it down, and HarperCollins and Transworld. It had been rejected by twelve publishing houses when it turned up at Bloomsbury, which had only just opened its children's book division, headed by Barry Cunningham (whose previous job, significantly, had been in the marketing division). And he had no doubt about the quality of the book: 'It was just terribly exciting. What struck me first was that the book came with a fully imagined world. There was a complete sense of Jo knowing the characters and what would happen to them.' Within a month, Bloomsbury had made an offer for the book, Christopher Little recommended its acceptance, and a delighted Rowling signed the contract, for an advance of £1,500 ($2,700). The book was eventually published under the name J.K. Rowling, because Christopher Little believed that, while girls read books by male authors, boys don't read them if they are written by women.

The celebration lunch took place at one of those Soho joints that publishers frequent, during which Barry gave Rowling his final piece of immortally sagacious advice: 'You'll never make any money out of children's books, Jo.'

It is now reckoned that, by the time of publication of the seventh Potter book, and the release of the seventh film, with the add-ons of Harry Potter computer games and assorted knick-knacks, Rowling will have earned a billion pounds. It didn't happen all at once – it never does – but it built inexorably. Bloomsbury printed a modest 500 copies of the first edition, but American rights were sold to Scholastic for $100,000, and Rowling found herself making headlines. The book received almost universally favourable reviews. Royalties usually build up slowly, and by the time of publication of the second of the series, *Harry Potter and the Chamber of Secrets*, Rowling had only pocketed cheques for £2,800 ($5,100). Only two years later, though, the four Harrys occupied places 1 – 4 in *The New York Times* bestselling list, and the royalties were over twenty million pounds (eleven million US dollars) a year. No book in the history of publishing has sold so well, so quickly. Everyone seems to love Harry Potter: not just the eight- to thirteen-year-old audience, for whom it was intended, but millions of adults who found themselves reading the books to their children, and enjoying them as much as the kids did.

And a vast number of adults who just read them for the sheer pleasure of it.

A certain number of these adults, it seems, were book collectors. They wanted first editions of the series, and they particularly wanted *Harry Potter and the Philosopher's Stone*. Within a year of publication, copies were changing hands at £500 ($900). Sheer madness, you might think. I thought so. Wrong, because the market for once was being driven by the collectors, and not by the rare book trade. There simply weren't enough of those first Harrys to go around, and prices rose precipitously. A recent copy at auction fetched £13,000 ($23,500), and I have seen them catalogued for as much as £25,000 ($45,000). For that price, for God's sake, you can buy a pretty good *collection* of W.B. Yeats, or Conrad, or D.H. Lawrence.

I made this point, a trifle forcibly, to *The Independent* columnist John Walsh, when he visited my office with a proof of the book, which he wished to sell.

'Please,' I begged him, 'Go away. I don't want it. Don't make me buy it.'

'C'mon,' he said firmly, 'how much?'

'Couple of thousand,' I said, 'but you'll do better elsewhere.'

He agreed. A few days later, sure enough, a long article appeared, tracing his journey round the book trade, getting offers for the proof. He eventually did considerably better than my paltry offer, and still had the grace to describe me as 'ebullient and wavy-haired'. I spent the next week flipping my hair this way and that, and emoting like crazy. And I still haven't dealt in the Harry Potter market.

Despite my disdain, the boy magician has had the same unprecedented, phenomenal effect in the rare book market as he has with the trade publications and movies. And what I'm still not clear about is: why? What is it about this unassuming little fellow, with his scarred forehead, that has so captivated audiences from Kettering to Kathmandu? I've read the books with enjoyment and admiration, but it's hard to understand why they have become so universally adored. They are a cunning amalgam of known – and freely admitted – sources: of Roald Dahl and C.S. Lewis, and knowingly yoke together traditional tales of sorcery with the going-away-to-school story. Somehow, though, the whole has become more than the sum of the parts. The books seem to have been touched by magic. Gold, gold, everything has turned to gold.

I wonder if Joanne Rowling, like King Midas before her, has any regrets, if she misses the life of diligent obscurity left behind in Edinburgh? Her daughter's first words were 'Harry Potter', which seems sad, and her father has sold the inscribed copies of the books she gave him, which apparently infuriated Rowling. There have been indications that the pleasures of endless rounds of publicity stunts and marketing gimmicks have palled. Faced with a day standing in front of a platform 9 3/4 installed at King's Cross, a grumpy Rowling said it was 'rather mad', and looked as if she wanted to disappear through that magic portal. And, of course, there's been the kickback that comes with success in England: the George Best mockers, Hugh Grant sniffers, Martin Amis tooth-pullers. There's nothing the English enjoy more than taking a famous person down a peg or two. Until they retire, of course, when they are regarded fondly. Think of Ian Botham or Ted Heath.

Attacks on Rowling have become common, but they must bewilder her nonetheless. She hasn't shown off, has avoided public appearances, simply got on with the work of pleasing tens of millions of children. Not enough, says critic and biographer Anthony Holden, who was one of the Whitbread Prize judges in 2000 and hated Ms Rowling's work. 'I found myself struggling to finish a tedious, badly-written version of Billy Bunter on broomsticks.' And the idea, playfully mooted round the internet, that she should be given the Nobel Prize for Literature does not amuse him in the least: 'JK Rowling winning the Nobel Prize for Literature makes about as much sense to me as Henry Kissinger winning the Nobel Peace prize.'

Well, that's a little mean, but it seemed positively generous when A.S. Byatt, herself a high quality mocker, entered the ring with a virulent attack on Rowling in *The New York Times*. The books were most admired, she argued, by those (children or adults) 'whose imaginative lives are confined to TV cartoons, and the exaggerated – more exciting, less threatening – mirror worlds of soaps, reality TV and celebrity gossip'. Anyone making serious claims for the Potter series was a semi-literate 'inhabitant of the urban jungle'.

The Harry Potter books are wildly popular, as Holden and Byatt allow, and regret. But this does not necessarily mean they are any good. Are the books, they ask urgently, *literature* in the honorific sense of the term? I don't want to argue here about what literature is, because an ostensive definition will do. *The Hobbit* is literature, and *The Famous Five* is not. Enid Blyton is part of our cultural heritage, not our literary one.

And where would one place J.K. Rowling? (And: does it matter?) I do not believe that such decisions are merely matters of taste. If you like Enid Blyton better than Tolkien, that's fine with me; if you think she is a better writer than Tolkien, you're either a very unsophisticated child, or an idiot.

You learn to make such discriminations, I think, by reading a lot, and by placing one thing beside another. I have, for instance, changed my view of the Harry Potter books since reading Philip Pullman's surpassingly brilliant trilogy, *His Dark Materials*. The Pullman series, like that of Rowling, has at its centre the question of the fate of the Universe. The battle between good and evil is, in both books, ultimately to be decided through the strength and faith of child protagonists. But if you put the two authors side by side, there is no doubt that Pullman is better, deeper, richer, and more demanding. *His Dark Materials* is a classic of our literature, and the Harry Potter series, I suspect, is not.

This doesn't bother me much, any more than it bothers me that Beethoven is better than the Beatles, or Keats than Bob Dylan. There's a lot of fun to be had out there, and a lot of ways to have it. I suspect that the hostility to J.K. Rowling comes down to simple numbers, and the envy that her astonishing career can generate. She is now the richest woman author in history, and made £125 ($225) million last year alone. Her books have been translated into sixty-one languages, and sold 230 million copies world-wide. All this in just seven years. Even Rowling allows that 'amazing' is too weak a term to account for it. 'Magical' is probably more accurate, as King Midas would testify.

HIGH WINDOWS

Over the years, one gets used to buying, selling, rebuying and reselling, the same book. Collectors get bored, change their interests, redeploy their resources, and I often reacquire a book I sold many years before. This rarely happens with manuscripts, though. The market is narrower, and most of the letters and manuscripts that we offer seem to end up in libraries, which are the right place for them. I rather resent it when rare books end up in public institutions, where they are likely to be both undervalued, and under-read. Manuscripts, though, can have research value, and should in general be made available to scholars.

Recently, however, I have tried to reacquire a little manuscript poem of Philip Larkin's, which I sold five or six years ago to the dealer Roy Davids, who had been unable to sell it. Since he is a much better seller of manuscripts than I, it would have been a seriously irrational repurchase. Once you know the contents of the poem, however, you will wonder why I wanted it back. I do too.

Entitled 'How to Win the Next Election', the poem (written in 1970) is intended to be sung to the tune of *Lillibullero*:

> Prison for strikers,
> Bring back the cat,
> Kick out the niggers –
> What about that?
> (Chos: niggers, niggers, etc.)
>
> Trade with the Empire,
> Ban the obscene,
> Lock up the Commies –
> God save the Queen.
> (Chos: commies, commies, etc.)

In his biography of Larkin, Andrew Motion cites this 'sour light verse' as incontrovertible evidence of Larkin's increasingly right-wing views, noting also his later poem (1977) 'On Her Majesty's Silver Jubilee':

> After Healey's trading figures,
> After Wilson's squalid crew
> And the rising tide of niggers
> What a treat, to look at you!

Larkin, of course, published neither of these, nor did his editor Anthony Thwaite see fit to include them in the *Collected Poems* in 1988. Thwaite classes such work as 'squibs, limericks and the like, which Larkin wrote in letters to his friends', noting that in the forthcoming *Selected Letters* 'they will be seen properly in context'. Thwaite (a life-time friend of the poet's) understood that poems like these, which were sent to old chums like Robert Conquest or Kingsley Amis, were understood by both author and recipient to be jokes, and *private*, as private as the letters in which they were included.

I'm not sure that this gets us – or Larkin – out of difficulty, quite. Surely sentiments like these are as offensive when voiced privately as publicly, though less likely to do harm. But ought they even to be classified as sentiments? Or what, exactly? The question one keeps coming back to is simple, and very difficult: is this Larkin's own voice, or that of some alter ego invented to amuse himself and his friends?

One thinks, in this context, of Barry Humphries' invention, Dame Edna Everage, and her mock-diatribes against cripples, pensioners, and 'tinted people'. Much offence might be taken about this, and Edna's way of deflecting it has been (brilliantly) to end each such outrage with 'And I mean that in the most caring way, possums.'

Is Edna a racist and a bigot? No, Edna is a parody of racists and bigots. Any idiot can see that. And as to Barry Humphries? Edna is his monster, not him, and he shows no signs of sharing her attitudes.

With Larkin the division of personae is by no means so clearly demarcated. There's no denying that Larkin was personally enraged by what he saw as the deterioration in the quality of English life in the late 1960s. Of Harold Wilson's Labour government he had written to Kingsley Amis in 1969: 'the decimal-loving, nigger-mad, army-cutting, abortion-promoting, murderer-pardoning, daylight-hating ponces, to hell with them, the worst government I can remember.' (He does not add that he says this in a caring way.) The letter was not intended for publication, admittedly, but let's be fair: not *not* intended for publication either, since by 1969 Larkin (and Amis) would have been fully aware that their letters might one day be subject to public scrutiny. So Larkin was presumably prepared, as it were, to come out into the open.

Or was he?

Let's go back to my little manuscript. I'd be surprised if some of my readers didn't smirk, however uneasily, reading it. It also makes you wince. I am reasonably sure, in my own case, that if you substituted 'Jews' for 'niggers' the impulse to snigger would go, and the wince would remain. Yet I would appear to have enough of the residual naughty schoolboy in me to relish a neat example of saying the unsayable. As Larkin put it, in a letter to the Warden of all Souls,

John Sparrow: 'we live in an odd era, when shocking language can be used, yet still shocks – it won't last . . . Or it can be funny, in that silly traditional way that such things are funny.'

Do we think Philip Larkin would have been rude to a black person he met? No. Given a chance, would he, like Enoch Powell, have repatriated black immigrants? I don't think so. Given a chance to express how much he hated the direction of modern life, might he playfully have taken on the tones of a passionate, bigoted Little Englander? No doubt about it. He could do it sufficiently well as to be indistinguishable from a bigoted lout, save for the level of wit and articulation. He was a superb mimic and irreverently opposed to the politically correct (even before that term had been invented), having fun striking outrageous attitudes for his friends. To ask whether he actually held such opinions would be to miss the point.

I *think* that's right.

I am sure, though, that the vulgarity in the 'squibs' we have been considering was an integral part of Larkin's nature: that it served as the (very) raw material that he could occasionally, alchemically, transform into great poetry. Perhaps there is something to be learned from citing the title poem of the volume *High Windows*, which was written at much the same period. You will remember that the poem, famously, begins with the lines:

> When I see a couple of kids
> And I guess he's fucking her and she's
> Taking pills or wearing a diaphragm,
> I know this is paradise

Though there seems to be the same common tone and easy vulgarity as the squibs from the letters, this is actually from a completely different register of thought and feeling. The tentative, old-maidishness of the perception 'taking pills' deliberately misconstrues 'on the pill', and the 'wearing' of the diaphragm suggests a pullover rather than a contraceptive device. There is a wistfulness and unease in the perception that suggests a man who, instead of railing at the world, feels uneasily separate from it, insecure and alone.

Larkin's capacity to bring together something (apparently) common with the genuinely sublime made *High Windows*, on its publication in 1974, his bestselling collection. Previously he had published a couple of books of poetry with small presses, but only one (*The Whitsun Weddings*, 1964) through a mainstream publisher, Faber and Faber. In June of 1973, Larkin wrote to his editor Charles Monteith, enclosing a small selection of poems, diffidently saying, 'I am not asking for it to be published so much as sending it to you for you to look at.'

Within two weeks, Monteith had agreed to publish, and immediately began to seek a new American publisher for the volume. Larkin's previous American books had done badly, which may have accounted for his opinion that 'American publishers are Neanderthal blockheads.' That view may well have been reinforced when Robert Giroux, who wished to publish the book, wanted to omit the poem 'Posterity' on the grounds that its references to 'Tel-Aviv', 'Myra's folks', and making 'the money sign' might be construed as anti-Semitic. For some months there was an impasse, but Larkin dug his heels in, the poem was included, and nobody died.

High Windows was published by Faber and Faber on 3 June 1974, in an edition of 6,000 copies, which is a large print run for a book of poetry. A further 7,500 copies followed in September, and another 6,000 in January. All of a sudden, from having been respected, Larkin was hugely admired, even loved. Reviews were consistently enthusiastic, though Larkin was not so much pleased, as relieved. There were kind words from the usual gang – Amis, Brownjohn, Nye, Wain – but it was Clive James's laudatory review in *Encounter* that seemed to give Larkin most pleasure. 'I think it is amazing,' he wrote to Anthony Thwaite, 'that such a tough egg as Clive James can find time for my old-maidish reservations, and I was much heartened by the unaffected and generous sympathy of his review.'

Sadly, *High Windows* was Larkin's last book, though he lived for another eleven years, and managed to squeeze out a few final, occasional bits of poems. But the light had gone out, and couldn't be rekindled – a process that is more commonly to be observed with romantic poets. After the publication of *High Windows*, he told Barbara Pym, it was impossible to write any more: 'the notion of expressing sentiments in short lines having similar sounds at their ends seems as remote as mangoes on the moon.'

Offered the office of Poet Laureate in 1984, he declined, already regarding himself as an ex-poet. His only regret at turning down the honour was that it might allow Ted Hughes – whom he once described as 'looking like a Christmas present from Easter Island' – whose poetry he loathed, to be appointed instead. 'The thought of Ted's being buried in Westminster Abbey is hard to live with. "There is regret. Always there is regret." Smoking can damage your bum.'

The first edition of *High Windows* isn't particularly valuable: £80 ($145) will buy you a nice copy. But it is uncommon with an inscription, since Larkin tended to reserve inscriptions for his friends, who have kept them. But occasionally one comes on the market, sometimes in the most peculiar way. In 1983 I catalogued a copy of *High Windows* with the inscription 'For Harold [Pinter] remembering his kindness in enabling me to have net practice – With kindest regards – Philip.' According to Anthony Thwaite, Larkin and Pinter 'shared a great interest in and enthusiasm for cricket,' and one of Larkin's letters to Pinter mentions getting up at 6.00 a.m. to listen to test matches, presumably from abroad.

I bought the book from the fabled book scout Martin Stone, in those days a cocaine-raddled, beret-wearing, tooth-decaying rock and roller who had discovered in early middle age a considerable talent for scouting out obscure and valuable books. He had purchased it at an auction of the effects of Pinter's ex-wife, the actress Vivien Merchant, who committed suicide in 1982, two years after their divorce.

My Catalogue Number 2 (1983) offered the book at £275 ($500) (it would be worth ten times that now). A couple of weeks after the catalogue came out, I received a phone call from Harold Pinter's secretary. Mr Pinter, she informed me, was angry and embarrassed that a book 'stolen from him' should be offered publicly for sale. I must send it back, immediately!

'I can quite understand that he is upset,' I said, 'given the circumstances. Let me have a word with him and I will see how I can help.'

Mr Pinter declined to speak to me, but was most chagrined to be told – you could hear the whispers and mutters as the secretary consulted him – that the book was sold.

'Mr Pinter wishes to know where you got it and who bought it. He insists it is his property!'

I explained that it had come from Vivien Merchant's

estate (whisper, whisper: silence) and that I had bought it from Martin Stone and sold it to the New York dealer Glenn Horowitz, giving both their phone numbers.

I was unhappy to be unwittingly caught in the middle like this, and could understand that, from Pinter's point of view, I must seem a little dodgy. Given that the book was inscribed to him, his contention that it was his was more than plausible; how it ended up with Vivien is a matter of conjecture. But it can be deeply embarrassing when a book inscribed to you comes (through no design of your own) onto the open market.

I tried to recover the book from Glenn, who told me that he had sold it to a private customer who loved it, and would under no price or circumstance sell it back.

A couple of weeks later there was another phone call, Pinter's secretary sounding distinctly on edge.

'Mr Gekoski,' she said accusingly, 'this Martin Stone doesn't answer his phone, and Mr Horowitz says the book is now sold to one of his customers . . .'

'Sounds right to me,' I said helpfully. 'Martin never answers the phone, and Glenn always sells the books. If I might speak to Mr Pinter perhaps I could explain further.'

Mr Pinter apparently hated the very idea of speaking to me. I wished him luck, and suggested he drop round to Martin Stone's flat and wait to see if he came home (which he did every now and then).

A few days later, the phone rang again. Mr Pinter was incandescent, according to his poor old secretary, and demanded restitution.

'I'd be happy to have a chat with him,' I said, 'because I am not sure what restitution I can make. Surely he doesn't want the money? He is welcome to it. But the book, sadly, is not going to come back.'

Mr Pinter, I gathered, would rather have died than talk to me.

'In that case,' I said, 'since he won't talk to me, and there's nothing else I can do, would you relay a message to him?'

'Yes,' the poor woman said wearily, she would be happy to.

'Tell him I'm sorry, but I'm sick to death of this, and to leave me alone!'

'There's no need to take that tone!' she announced grandly (whisper, whisper, grunt), on which unresolved note we hung up simultaneously, never to speak again.

I'm rather embarrassed to admit to this bit of blatant rudeness. In general I'm unrelentingly nice to famous playwrights. Tom Stoppard, I'll bet, wouldn't hear a word said against me. But I can't always magic books back once they're gone.

Since that time, I have handled a lot of Larkin material – a published letter of his from 1984 notes that 'he [that's me] sells my books at huge prices' – but I haven't had another inscribed *High Windows*. I'm rather relieved, really. They're more trouble than they are worth.

Fortunately, Roy Davids had sold the manuscript of 'How to Win the Next Election'. I'm not clear why I wanted to repurchase it, when there are so many more attractive things to buy. For some obscure reason, that little piece of paper works on my feelings, stimulates and frustrates me, as if it were some sort of hieroglyph that, properly deciphered, would give me the key to poor old Philip Larkin.

It is uncomfortably closer to the truth, I suspect, that 'How to Win the Next Election' is more touch-stone than talisman. What it reveals is something about those who come into contact with it. Though I greatly dislike Andrew Motion's po-faced dismissal of this side of Larkin, I don't much respect my own capacity to read the poem and to snigger, however disapprovingly. I'm glad Roy sold it, and I don't envy its new owner the pleasure of its company.